PENGUIN INTERNATIONAL POETS

CONTEMPORARY AMERICAN POETRY

D0026940

CONTEMPORARY
AMERICAN POETRY

EDITED BY
DONALD HALL

Second Edition
(Revised and Expanded)

PENGUIN BOOKS

PENGUIN BOOKS

Published by the Penguin Group
27 Wrights Lane, London w8 5TZ, England
Viking Penguin Inc., 40 West 23rd Street, New York, New York 10010, USA
Penguin Books Australia Ltd, Ringwood, Victoria, Australia
Penguin Books Canada Ltd, 2801 John Street, Markham, Ontario, Canada L3R 1B4
Penguin Books (NZ) Ltd, 182–190 Wairau Road, Auckland 10, New Zealand

Penguin Books Ltd, Registered Offices: Harmondsworth, Middlesex, England

First published 1962
Reprinted 1964, 1965, 1966, 1967, 1968, 1969, 1970, 1971
Second edition (revised and expanded) 1972
Reprinted 1972, 1974, 1976, 1977, 1979, 1980, 1982, 1983,
1984, 1986, 1987, 1988

Printed and bound in Great Britain by
Cox & Wyman Ltd, Reading
Set in Monotype Fournier

CONTENTS

WILLIAM STAFFORD (b. 1914) comes from Kansas and was educated at the universities of Kansas, Wisconsin and Iowa. He has taught in California and Indiana and is now at Lewis and Clark College in Oregon. *West of Your City* appeared in 1960, and *Travelling Through the Dark* (winner of the National Book Award) in 1962. In 1966 he published *The Rescued Year* and in 1970 *Allegiances.*

DUDLEY RANDALL (b. 1914) is a librarian in Detroit, and publisher of the Broadside Press, which prints broadsides and books by black American poets. Randall published some of his poems, together with poems by Margaret Danner, in *Poem Counterpoem* (1966), and a second collection, *Cities Burning*, in 1968.

CONTENTS

DAVID IGNATOW (b. 1914) has lived most of his life in Manhattan. In 1961 he published *Say Pardon*, and in 1964 *Figures of the Human*, which collected poems from volumes that had gone out of print. *Rescue the Dead*, from which all of these poems are taken, was published in 1968. In 1970 he published *Poems 1934–1969*.

ROBERT LOWELL (1917–77) was a member of the Bostonian family that included a president of Harvard and the poets Amy and James Russell. He attended Harvard and Kenyon and studied with John Crowe Ransom. *Lord Weary's Castle* (1946), Lowell's first full-scale book, won the Pulitzer Prize for Poetry in 1947. *The Mills of the Kavanagh's* followed in 1951, and *Life Studies* (which won the National Book Award) in 1959. A book of translations, *Imitations*, appeared in 1961, and a translation of Racine's *Phedre* in 1961. He published a new collection of poems, *For the Union Dead*, in 1964 and a collection of his plays, *The Old Glory*, in 1965. His most recent collections of poems are *Near the Ocean* (1967), *Notebooks* (1969), a revised *Notebook* 1970, *For Lizzie and Harriet* (1973), *History* (1973), and *The Dolphin* (1973).

ROBERT DUNCAN (b. 1919) comes from Oakland, California, and has continued to live near by. He has edited the *Experimental Review* and *Phoenix*, and taught at Black Mountain College and the University of Buffalo. Among his books are *The Opening of the Field* (1960), *Roots and Branches* (1964) and *Bending the Bow* (1968).

REED WHITTEMORE (b. 1919) was born in New Haven, Connecticut, and attended Yale University. He taught at Carleton College, was consultant in poetry at the Library of Congress in 1964–65, and is now on the staff of the National Institute of Public Affairs in Washington, D.C. He has published six volumes of poetry, of which the most recent is *Poems New and Selected* (1967).

HOWARD NEMEROV (b. 1920), joined the Royal Canadian Air Force after graduating from Harvard, and flew in England during the Second World War. He has published considerable literary criticism, three novels, a book of short stories and an autobiographical *Journal of the Fictive Life*, as well as several books of poems. *New and Selected Poems* appeared in 1960 and was followed by *The Next Room of the Dream* (1962) and *The Blue Swallows* (1967).

RICHARD WILBUR (b. 1921) was educated at Amherst College and Harvard, where he took an M.A. in 1947, and was a Junior Fellow in the Society of Fellows 1947–50. He has taught at Harvard, Wellesley and Wesleyan University, and he has been a Guggenheim Fellow and received a Prix de Rome. His books of poems include *The Beautiful Changes* (1947), *Ceremony* (1950), *Things of this World* (1956), *Poems 1943–1956* (1957) and *Advice to a Prophet* (1961). In 1957 he received the Pulitzer Prize and the National Book Award for *Things of this World*. He is also an accomplished translator, especially known for his translation of plays by Molière, *The Misanthrope* (1955) and *Tartuffe* (1963). In 1969 he published a new collection of poems, *Walking to Sleep.*

ANTHONY HECHT (b. 1922) is a native of New York City, and attended Kenyon College, where he studied with John Crowe Ransom. He has taught at Smith College, Bard, and the University of Rochester. He has been a Guggenheim Fellow and Hudson Review Fellow. *A Summoning of Stones* appeared in 1954, and *The Hard Hours* (which included a selection from the earlier book) was published in 1967 and received the Pulitzer Prize.

JAMES DICKEY (b. 1923) was born in Georgia and has lived most of his life in the South. He has been a Guggenheim Fellow, consultant in poetry for the Library of Congress, and teaches at the University of South Carolina. In 1967 he gathered his verse together in *Poems 1957–67*. In 1968 he collected his criticism under the title *From Babel to Byzantium.* His most recent collection of poems is *Eye-*

DENISE LEVERTOV (b. 1923) comes from Ilford in
Essex, England, and served as a nurse during the Second
World War, when her poems were first published by Wrey
Gardiner in London. She married the American writer,
Mitchell Goodman, and has lived in the United States since
1948. Her American books include *Here and Now* (1957),
Overland to the Islands (1958), *With Eyes at the Back of our
Heads* (1960), *The Jacob's Ladder* (1961), *O Taste and See!*
(1964), *The Sorrow Dance* (1967) and *Relearning the
Alphabet* (1970).

JOHN LOGAN (b. 1923) is editor of *Choice*, and teaches at
the University of Buffalo. His books of poems are *Cycle
for Mother Cabrini* (1955), *Ghosts of the Heart* (1960),
Spring of the Thief (1963) and *Zigzag Walk: Poems 1963–
1968* (1969).

LOUIS SIMPSON (b. 1923), born in Jamaica in the West
Indies, came to the United States in 1940, and attended
Columbia University. He spent three years in the United
States Army, mostly in the glider infantry, and received
his citizenship at Berchtesgaden. He has been a publisher,

9

and has taught at the University of California, Berkeley and at Stony Brook in Long Island. He has published a novel, a critical book and six books of poems. *At the End of the Open Road* won the Pulitzer Prize in 1964, *Selected Poems* appeared in 1966 and *The Adventures of the Letter I* in 1971.

EDGAR BOWERS (b. 1924) was born in Georgia, and attended the University of North Carolina and Stanford, where he studied with Yvor Winters. He has been a Sewanee Review Fellow and a Guggenheim Fellow. He now teaches at the University of California, Santa Barbara. His books of poems are *The Form of Loss* (1956) and *The Astronomers* (1965).

JOHN HAINES (b. 1924) was born in Virginia, and in the late forties studied painting and sculpture in Washington and New York. He went to Alaska in 1947, and lived in a cabin which he built himself some seventy miles from Fairbanks. He published *Winter News* in 1966 and *The Stone Harp* in 1971.

CONTENTS

CONTENTS

ROBERT CREELEY (b. 1926) was raised in Massachusetts, attended Harvard, and served in India and Burma with the American Field Service during the war. Later he lived in France, Spain and Guatemala, where he edited and taught school. He has taught at Black Mountain College, at the University of New Mexico and now at San Francisco State. He has published a novel and a book of short stories, as well as several volumes of poetry. His poems are available in three volumes, *For Love* (1962), *Words* (1967) and *Pieces* (1969).

JAMES MERRILL (b. 1926) is a graduate of Amherst College and lives in Stonington, Connecticut. He has published two novels and several books of poems, including *Nights and Days*, which won the National Book Award in 1967. *Poems 1948–1961* appeared in England in 1962. *The Fire Screen* appeared in 1969.

W. D. SNODGRASS (b. 1926) grew up in Beaver Falls, Pennsylvania, where he majored in music at Geneva College. After service in the Navy he attended the State University of Iowa, and taught at Cornell, Rochester and Wayne State University in Detroit. He is now teaching at Syracuse University. His first book of poems, *Heart's Needle* (1959), received a Pulitzer Prize in 1960. In 1968 he published *After Experience*.

A. R. AMMONS (b. 1926) was born in Whiteville, North
Carolina. After many years in business, Ammons took a
position teaching at Cornell University. He has published
six books of poems, including *Selected Poems* (1968),
Uplands (1970) and *Briefings* (1971).

ALLEN GINSBERG (b. 1926) was born in Paterson, New
Jersey, the son of a school teacher and poet. He attended
Columbia College, and with the publication of *Howl* in
1957 he became a spiritual leader of the young in America.
Kaddish (1961) was his next collection, followed by
Reality Sandwiches (1963) and *Planet News* in 1968.

JOHN WOODS (b. 1926) was born in Martinsville, Indiana,
and teaches at Western Michigan University. He is the
author of books of poetry, including *The Cutting Edge*
(1966), *Keeping out of Trouble* (1968) and *Turning to Look
Back: Poems 1955–1970* (1971).

CONTENTS

FRANK O'HARA (1926–66) grew up in New England and attended Harvard and the University of Michigan, where he won a Hopwood Award. Most of his adult life he spent in New York, one of the group of poets associated with contemporary painters. He worked for *Art News* and The Museum of Modern Art, where he was an assistant curator of exhibitions at the time of his accidental death. The Museum published a posthumous collection of his poems illustrated by painters who were his friends, *In Memory of My Feelings*. In 1971, Knopf published *The Collected Poems of Frank O'Hara*.

JOHN ASHBERY (b. 1927), a native of Sodus, New York, was educated at Deerfield and Harvard. He has worked for *Art News* and been art critic for the Paris edition of the *New York Herald Tribune*. He has published four principal collections of poems, *Some Trees* (Yale Series of Younger Poets, 1956), *The Tennis Court Oath* (1962), *Rivers and Mountains* (1966) and *The Double Dream of Spring* (1970).

GALWAY KINNELL (b. 1927) was born in Rhode Island and attended Princeton University. He has lived in France, where he taught at Grenoble, and in Iran. He has translated Yves Bonnefoy and Villon, among other French poets. He lives in an old farmhouse in Vermont, from which he occasionally departs to teach for a semester or two. He has published *What a Kingdom It Was* (1960), *Flower Herding on Mount Monadnock* (1964), *Body Rags* (1968) and *The Book of Nightmares* (1971).

W. S. MERWIN (b. 1927) was born in New York City, raised
in Pennsylvania, and educated at Princeton University. He
has spent most of the last two decades in Spain, England
and France, where he has a small cottage. He has pub-
lished numerous translations from Spanish and French. His
seven books of poems include *The Drunk in the Furnace*
(1960), *The Moving Target* (1963), *The Lice* (1967) and
The Carrier of Ladders (1970).

JAMES WRIGHT (b. 1927) is a native of Ohio, and studied
under John Crowe Ransom and Theodore Roethke. He
has been a Kenyon Review Fellow, and has lived in Austria
on a Fulbright Award. He taught at the University of
Minnesota and now teaches at Hunter College in New
York. His books of poems are *The Green Wall* (Yale Series
of Younger Poets, 1957), *Saint Judas* (1959), *The Branch
Will Not Break* (1963), *Shall We Gather at the River*
(1968). His *Collected Poems* appeared in 1971.

ANNE SEXTON (1928–74) began writing poems in 1957. *To Bedlam and Part Way Back* appeared in 1960, followed by *All My Pretty Ones* (1962), *Live or Die*, which won the Pulitzer Prize in 1967, *Transformations* (1971), *Book of Folly* (1972), and *The Death Notebooks* (1974).

DONALD HALL (b. 1928) is editor of this anthology. He was born in Connecticut, and since 1957 has lived in Ann Arbor, Michigan. He spent two years at Oxford on a Henry Fellowship, and has returned to spend two more years in England subsequently. His books of poems include *Exiles and Marriages* (1955), *The Dark Houses* (1958), *A Roof of Tiger Lilies* (1963), *The Alligator Bride* (1969) and *The Yellow Room love poems* (1971).

X. J. KENNEDY (b. 1929) is a native of New Jersey and took his B.A. at Seton Hall University, going to the University of Michigan for graduate study. His first book of poems, *Nude Descending a Staircase*, was the Lamont Poetry Selection for 1961. He teaches at Tufts University. In 1969 he published a second book of poems, *Growing Into Love*.

CONTENTS

17

Shortly after the birth of her second child in 1962, she wrote
the poems of her posthumous volume, *Ariel* (1965).

ETHERIDGE KNIGHT (b. 1933) was born in Corinth,
Mississippi. He has written of himself, 'I died in Korea
from a shrapnel wound and narcotics resurrected me. I
died in 1960 from a prison sentence and poetry brought
me back to life.' His book of poems is called *Poems from
Prison*, and appeared in 1968. He was released from the
Indiana State Prison in December 1968.

MICHAEL BENEDIKT (b. 1937) lives in New York. *The
Body* was published in 1968, *Sky* in 1970 and *Mole Notes*
in 1971. He has also published considerable translation.

TOM CLARK (b. 1941) grew up in Chicago and was grad-
uated from the University of Michigan in 1963, where he
won a Major Hopwood Award for poetry. He then
attended Cambridge University and the University of
Essex, returning to the United States in 1967. He now lives
in California. His first major collection of poems, *Stones*,
appeared in 1969 and *Air* in 1970.

RON PADGETT (b. 1942) was born in Tulsa, Oklahoma, and edited a magazine while he was still in high school which included work by Allen Ginsberg, Robert Creeley and LeRoi Jones. With several other artists from Tulsa, he moved to New York, and currently lives in the East Village. His book of collaborations with Ted Berrigan, *Bean Spasms*, appeared in 1967. In 1969 he published a collection of his own poems, called *Great Balls of Fire*.

ACKNOWLEDGEMENTS

For permission to publish or reproduce the poems in this anthology, acknowledgement is made to the following:

For A. R. AMMONS: 'Hymn', 'Terrain' and 'Prospecting' were first published in the *Hudson Review*, and have subsequently appeared in his *Expressions of Sea Level* (Columbus: Ohio State University Press, 1963) and *Selected Poems* (Ithaca, New York: Cornell University Press, 1968), Copyright © 1957, 1960 by A. R. Ammons. For 'Loss', Copyright © 1964 by A. R. Ammons. Reprinted from *Corson's Inlet*, Copyright © 1965 by Cornell University. Used by permission of Cornell University Press.

For JOHN ASHBERY: to the author and Yale University Press for 'The Picture of Little J. A. in a Prospect of Flowers' and 'Some Trees', from *Some Trees*, and Wesleyan University Press for 'Thoughts of a Young Girl' and 'Our Youth', Copyright © John Ashbery 1962, from *The Tennis Court Oath* by John Ashbery.

For MICHAEL BENEDIKT: Copyright © 1965, 1967, 1968 by Michael Benedikt. Reprinted from *The Body* by Michael Benedikt by permission of Wesleyan University Press. 'The Eye' and 'Thoughts' were first published in *Poetry*.

For ROBERT BLY: to the author.

For EDGAR BOWERS: to the author and Alan Swallow, the publisher, for 'The Prince' and 'The Mountain Cemetery' from *The Form of Loss* by Edgar Bowers, Copyright © 1954 by Edgar Bowers.

For TOM CLARK: to the author and Harper & Row, Publishers, Inc. for 'Going to School in France or America', 'Poems', 'Doors' and 'Eyeglasses' from *Stones*, 1969, Copyright © 1967 by Tom Clark.

For ROBERT CREELEY: to the author and Charles Scribner's Sons for poems from *For Love* by Robert Creeley, Copyright © by Robert Creeley.

For JAMES DICKEY: to the author and Charles Scribner's Sons for 'The Performance', Copyright © 1959 by The Modern Poetry Society, from POETS OF TODAY VII, *Into the Stone and Other Poems* by James Dickey.

For EDWARD DORN: to the author and Corinth Books Inc. for 'Home on the Range, February 1962' and 'On the Debt My Mother Owed to Sears Roebuck' from *Hands Up*, 1964, copyright © 1964 by Edward Dorn Totem Press/Corinth Books, and to Fulcrum Press for 'A Song' and 'Mourning Letter, March 29 1963' from *Geography*.

For ROBERT DUNCAN: to the author and Grove Press, Inc. for 'A Poem Beginning with a Line by Pindar' from *The Opening of the Field* by Robert Duncan, Copyright © 1960 by Robert Duncan.

For ALLEN GINSBERG: to the author and City Lights Books for 'A Supermarket in California' from *Howl*, 1956, 'Dream Record' from *Reality Sandwiches*, 1963, and 'To Lindsay', 'Message' and 'The End' from *Kaddish*, 1961, and Jonathan Cape Ltd for 'First Party at Ken Keseys' from *T.V. Baby Poems*, (*T.V. Baby Poems* is published in the U.S.A. by Grossman Publishers Inc.)

For JOHN HAINES: to the author and to Wesleyan University Press for 'And When the Green Man Comes', 1961, 'The Tundra', 1964, 'Foreboding', 1964, 'If the Owl Calls Again', 1962, 'To Turn Back', 1964 from *Winter News*, Copyright © 1961, 1962, 1964 by John Haines, reprinted from *Winter News* by John Haines, by permission of Wesleyan University Press.

For DONALD HALL: to the author.

For ANTHONY HECHT: to the author and The Macmillan Company for 'Samuel Sewall' and 'Alceste in the Wilderness' from *A Summoning of Stones* by Anthony Hecht.

For DAVID IGNATOW: to the author and Wesleyan University Press for 'The Bagel', 'Rescue the Dead', 'Ritual Three', 'East Bronx' and 'All Quiet' from *Rescue the Dead*, Copyright © 1964, 1966, 1967 by David Ignatow. Reprinted from *Rescue the Dead*, by David Ignatow, by permission of Wesleyan University Press. 'Rescue the Dead' and 'All Quiet' were first published in *Poetry*.

For DONALD JUSTICE: to the author and Wesleyan University Press for poems from *The Summer Anniversaries* by Donald Justice, Copyright © 1954, 1956, 1959 by Donald Justice.

For X. J. KENNEDY: to the author and Doubleday and Co. Inc. for poems from *Nude Descending a Staircase* by X. J. Kennedy, Copyright © 1960, 1961 by X. J. Kennedy.

For GALWAY KINNELL: to Houghton Mifflin Co. and the author.

For ETHERIDGE KNIGHT: to the author and Broadside Press for poems from *Poems in Prison*.

For DENISE LEVERTOV: to the author.

For JOHN LOGAN: to the author and the University of Chicago Press for 'The Picnic' and 'A Trip to Four or Five Towns', from *Ghosts of the Heart* by John Logan.

For ROBERT LOWELL: to Faber and Faber Ltd, the author, Farrar, Straus and Cudahy Inc. for poems from *Life Studies* by Robert Lowell, Copyright © Robert Lowell 1956, 1959, and Harcourt, Brace and World, Inc. for poems from *Lord Weary's Castle* by Robert Lowell, Copyright © 1956, 1959 by Robert Lowell.

For JAMES MERRILL: to the *New Yorker* and the author.

For W. S. MERWIN: to Rupert Hart-Davis, the author, and Harold Ober Associates Inc. for 'The Bones', Copyright © 1959, 'Small Woman on Swallow Street', and 'Grandfather in the Old Men's Home', Copyright © 1959. all from *The Drunk in the Furnace* by W. S. Merwin.

For FRANK O'HARA: to the author and the Estate for 'Why I am not a Painter' and to City Lights Books, for 'A Step Away from Them' and 'Steps' from *Lunch Poems*, 1964.

For RON PADGETT: to the author.

For SYLVIA PLATH: to the author and Olwyn Hughes, and to Harper & Row, Publishers, Inc. for 'Lady Lazarus', 'Death & Co.' and 'Words' from *Ariel*, Copyright © 1963 and 1965 Ted Hughes, reprinted by permission of Harper & Row Inc.

For DUDLEY RANDALL: to the author and Broadside Press for 'Roses and Revolutions' and 'Black Poet, White Critic' from *Cities Burning* and 'Old Witherington' and 'George' from *Poem Counterpoem*.

For HOWARD NEMEROV: to the Margot Johnson Agency and the author.

For ADRIENNE RICH: to the author and Harper and Brothers for 'The Insusceptibles', from *The Diamond Cutters and Other Poems* by Adrienne Rich, Copyright © Adrienne Rich Conrad 1955.

For ANNE SEXTON: to the author and Olwyn Hughes and Houghton Mifflin Co. for 'Lament' from *All My Pretty Ones*, 'Wanting to Die' from *Live or Die* and 'That Day' from *Love Poems*.

For LOUIS SIMPSON: to the author and Charles Scribner's Sons for 'The Ash and the Oak', Copyright © Louis Simpson 1951, and 'Early in the Morning', Copyright © Louis Simpson, 1955, from POETS OF TODAY II, *Good News of Death and other Poems*, by Louis Simpson, and to Wesleyan University Press for 'To the Western World', Copyright © 1957, from *A Dream of Governors* by Louis Simpson.

For W. D. SNODGRASS: to the author and Alfred A. Knopf Inc. for poems from *Heart's Needle* by W. D. Snodgrass, Copyright © 1959 by W. D. Snodgrass.

For GARY SNYDER: to Origin Press and the author.

For WILLIAM STAFFORD: to the author.

For REED WHITTEMORE: to the author and the University of Minnesota Press for 'Still Life' and 'A Day with the Foreign Legion', from *An American takes a Walk and Other Poems* by Reed Whittemore, Copyright © Reed Whittemore 1956, and The Macmillan Company for 'The Walk Home', 'On the Suicide of a Friend' and 'The Party', from *The Self Made Man* by Reed Whittemore, Copyright © Reed Whittemore 1956, 1958, 1959.

For RICHARD WILBUR: to Faber and Faber Ltd, the author, and Harcourt, Brace and World Inc. for 'Tywater', from *The Beautiful Changes and Other Poems* by Richard Wilbur, Copyright © Richard Wilbur 1947, for three poems from 'Ceremony', from *Ceremony and Other Poems* by Richard Wilbur, Copyright © 1948, 1949, 1950 by Richard Wilbur, and for 'After the Last Bulletins', Copyright © The *New Yorker* Magazine Inc. 1953, from *Things of this World* by Richard Wilbur.

ACKNOWLEDGEMENTS

For JOHN WOODS: to the author and Indiana University Press for poems from *Keeping Out of Trouble*.

For JAMES WRIGHT: to the author, Yale University Press for 'A Gesture by a Lady with an Assumed Name', from *The Green Wall*, and Wesleyan University Press for 'At Thomas Hardy's Birthplace, 1953', Copyright © 1957, and 'Saint Judas', Copyright © 1956, both from *Saint Judas* by James Wright.

INTRODUCTION

FOR thirty years an orthodoxy ruled American poetry. It derived from the authority of T. S. Eliot and the new critics; it exerted itself through the literary quarterlies and the universities. It asked for a poetry of symmetry, intellect, irony, and wit. The last few years have broken the control of this orthodoxy. The change has come slowly and not as a rebellion of young turks against old tories. For one thing, the orthodoxy produced many good poems and some of its members are still producing them. For another, much of the attack on it came from sources – like *Time* and the publicists of the Beat Generation – which could not supply literary alternatives to the orthodoxy.

Yet we must not regret the dissolution of the old government. In modern art anarchy has proved preferable to the restrictions of a benevolent tyranny. It is preferable as a permanent condition. We do not want merely to substitute one orthodoxy for another – Down with *Understanding Poetry*! Long Live *Projective Verse*! – but we want all possibilities, even contradictory ones, to exist together. The trouble with orthodoxy is that it prescribes the thinkable limits of variation; among young poets of the forties and fifties, almost without exception, surrealism was quite literally beyond consideration. The orthodoxy which prevailed in every literary context had decided, while the poet was still in short pants, that 'surrealism had failed'. And that was the end of that. Yet typically the modern artist has allowed nothing to be beyond his consideration. He has acted as if restlessness were a conviction and has destroyed his own past in order to create a future. He has said to himself, like the policeman to the vagrant, 'Keep moving.'

Modern American poetry began in London shortly after the death of Queen Victoria. Ezra Pound recalls that Conrad Aiken told him that there was 'a guy at Harvard doing funny stuff. Mr Eliot turned up a year or so later.' Harriet Monroe founded *Poetry* in 1912, and discovered Mr Pound on her neck encouraging her to print Eliot, Frost, and Yeats. But soon after the first successes of modernist poetry in America, when Amy Lowell was flying the flag of revolution, the modernists split into opposing camps. One side of this split became the orthodoxy that prevailed from, say, 1925 to 1955.

In the first decades of this century there were the expatriates and there were the poets who remained in the United States. Pound, Aiken, and Eliot congregated in London, but things were also going on in New York. Poets and editors like Alfred Kreymbourg, Mina Loy, William Carlos Williams, Marianne Moore, Wallace Stevens, E. E. Cummings, and Hart Crane mingled and established a domestic literary milieu. They shared little but liveliness and talent, but most of them also experimented with the use of common American speech, an indigenous language increasingly distinguishable from English. Even the frenchified Wallace Stevens and the rhetorical Hart Crane participated in this endeavour. And none of these New York poets shared the concern with history which occupied Eliot and Pound, or the erudition which this concern imposed.

Pound was the link between London and Greenwich Village, as editor and publicist and even as poet. But he was unable to reconcile the slangy Williams and the polyglot Eliot. And it was the ideas of Eliot which proved attractive to the young men who took power. According to William Carlos Williams in his *Autobiography*, '*The Waste Land* wiped out our world ... Eliot returned us to the classroom.' Eliot was never further from a colloquial language than at the end of the most famous poem of our modern literature:

London bridge is falling down falling down falling down
Poi s'ascose nel foco che gli affina
Quando fiam uti chelidon – O swallow swallow
Le Prince d' Aquitaine à la tour abolie
These fragments I have shored against my ruins
Why then Ile fit you. Hieronymo's mad againe.
Datta. Dayadhvam. Damyata.
    Shantih shantih shantih

It was not only a matter of language, however; and in some of his poems Eliot certainly used a vocabulary and a rhythm which were close to common American speech. Eliot's attitudes towards history and tradition were more deeply relevant, as well as his sense of the continuity of American and English poetry. Probably his influence was largely accomplished through his criticism. From the mid-twenties until very recently, American poetry has functioned as a part of the English tradition. The colloquial side of American literature – the side which valued 'experience' more than 'civilization' – was neglected by the younger poets. Melville said that the whaleboats of the Pacific had been his Harvard and his Yale College; Henry James crossed the Atlantic from Harvard to Lamb House. The directions are as contrary as East and West.

The new poets admired the forms of the sixteenth and seventeenth centuries, and themselves attempted to write a symmetrical and intellectual poetry which resembled Ralegh or Dryden more than 'Gerontion' or the *Cantos*. One can divide the chief poets of this time into those who admired the tough density of Donne, and those who preferred the wit of Marvell or the delicacy of Herrick. There were Allen Tate and Yvor Winters on the one hand, and there was John Crowe Ransom on the other. Late in the thirties another group of poets took their departure most obviously from Auden – Karl Shapiro and John Frederick Nims were the best, I think – but because their poems were witty and formal they did not depart from the general area of the orthodoxy.

Immediately after the war, two books were published which were culminations of the twin strains of density and delicacy. Robert Lowell's *Lord Weary's Castle* is a monument of the line of tough rhetoricians; beyond this it was impossible to go. (The failure of John Berryman's *Homage to Mistress Bradstreet*, as I see it, only proves my point.) The effect of tremendous power under tremendous pressure was a result of a constricted subject matter and a tense line, in which the strict decasyllable was counterbalanced by eccentric caesura and violent enjambement. In contrast was Richard Wilbur's *The Beautiful Changes*, which was the peak of skilful elegance. Here was the ability to shape an analogy, to perceive and develop comparisons, to display etymological wit, and to pun six ways at once. It appealed to the mind because it was intelligent, and to the sense of form because it was intricate and shapely. It did not appeal to the passions and it did not pretend to. These two poets, though they are not the oldest here, form the real beginning of post-war American poetry because they are the culmination of past poetries.

Lowell had his imitators, but they were not very successful because Lowell's style was idiosyncratic. Many poets after Wilbur resembled him, and some of them were good at it, but the typical *ghastly* poem of the fifties was a Wilbur poem not written by Wilbur, a poem with tired wit and obvious comparisons and nothing to keep the mind or the ear occupied. (It wasn't Wilbur's fault, though I expect he will be asked to suffer for it.) The *poème bien fait*, which filled the quarterlies of the fifties, was usually not that damned *bien fait*. Too often it sounded like:

> Also the wind assumed the careful day
> And down the avenues of hollow light
> The sons of Jupiter to their dismay
> Perceived the ritual desuetude of night.

The real subject of these poems was the faint music of their diction. They were decadent products of the old move toward irony, wit, and control. The experiments of 1927 became the clichés of 1952. American poetry, which has always been outrageous – compare Whitman and Dickinson to Browning and Tennyson – dwindled into long poems in iambics called 'Herakles: A Double Sestina'. Myth, myth, myth. Jung was perhaps influential, but what distinguished these poems from the fables of Edwin Muir was that they existed in order to *prevent* meaning. Nobody could pin them down. Sometimes it seemed that the influence of Senator McCarthy was stronger than that of Jung.

Meanwhile a series of contrary directions in poetry had existed in semi-obscurity. The vanguard *New Directions* annuals printed some of them, and others survived in little mimeographed magazines and home-made pamphlets. Most of these underground poems were bad, like most poems anywhere, but they were bad in ways differing from the prevailing badness. In the thirties there was a brief upsurge of surrealism, which produced nothing. There was also a certain amount of Marxist poetry, some of it publicized, but except for the sarcasms of Kenneth Fearing little of it was readable.

The only contrary direction which endured throughout the orthodoxy was the direction I will inadequately call the colloquial, or the line of William Carlos Williams. Williams himself has been admired by most new American poets, of whatever school, but the poets of the orthodoxy have admired him for his descriptive powers; they learned from him a conscience of the eye rather than a conscience of the ear; for Williams the problem of native speech rhythm was of first importance.

This poetry is no mere restriction of one's vocabulary. It wants to use the language with the intimacy acquired in unrehearsed unliterary speech. But it has other characteristics which are not linguistic. It is a poetry of experiences more than of ideas. The experience is presented often without comment, and the words of the description must supply the emotion which the experience generates, without generalization or summary. Often too this poetry finds great pleasure in the world outside. It is the poetry of a man in the world, responding to what he sees: with disgust, with pleasure, in rant and in meditation. Naturally, this colloquial direction makes much of accuracy, of honest speech. 'Getting the tone right' is the poet's endeavour, not 'turning that metaphor neatly', or 'inventing a new stanza'. Conversely, when it fails most commonly it fails because the emotion does not sound true.

People who had learned from Williams, and from Pound's structure and metric, had a hard time of it until the fifties. Then some good editors began to print the best of them, and the movement which had lapsed in the twenties came alive again. Cid Corman started *Origin* in 1951, and printed many of the best poems written in this tradition. Jonathan Williams started the Jargon Press in North Carolina, and printed good poets who were later picked up by New York publishers. I will not try to discriminate among the various poets who belong, some quite loosely, to this strain of American literature. Denise Levertov is from England, Robert Creeley from Massachusetts, Robert Duncan from California; the sources of their poetry are probably as varied as their geographical origins. All these poets and many more pay tribute to an older poet, Charles Olson, who in his letters, articles and poems (though he did not begin publishing until the fifties) erected a critical standard for them. But one thing unites them all: an alternative to the traditional poetry of the last decades was necessary, and was implicit in the nature of America; a Henry James demands a Herman Melville, an English influence begets a French antagonist.

When he wrote *Life Studies*, Robert Lowell sent his muse to the *atelier* of William Carlos Williams. Many of the poets of the orthodoxy have felt the need to move on, to change. Earlier than Lowell, Richard Eberhart and Theodore Roethke moved from their original old models to new unorthodoxies. (Others, like Richard Wilbur, are staying put, and there is no reason why a man should change if he doesn't feel like changing. There is Ezra Pound but there is also Robert Frost.) I suggested that *Lord Weary's Castle* was the culmination of one movement. *Life Studies* looks like an attempt at synthesis. If the poet of rhetorical stanzas can come closer to common speech, he may avoid the mere fabrication of mandalas into available shapes. The challenge of free verse is to make shapes which derive their identity by improvisation, without reference to past poems. And also, a new form can uncover or make possible a new subject matter. Synthesis of the literary and the colloquial occurs, surely, in some of the poets of the vanguard already. An approach of the two contraries may guard against the perversions of each.

I have not mentioned another group of poets who are sufficiently separate. (I have not mentioned the Beat Generation, incidentally, because it is an invention of weekly news magazines. Insofar as it has made several good lines of poetry, it has belonged to the colloquial tradition.) These are a group of New Yorkers who have been associated with Action Painting – some have worked for *Art News*, or the Museum of Modern Art – and whose poetry attempts a similar vitality. Their closeness to modern French poetry seems obvious. Frank O'Hara,* with his *Second Avenue*, comes closest to Action Writing. But the best of these poets, it seems to me, is John Ashbery, whom I print here.

Most of my comments have limited themselves to the terms of technique, like vocabulary and symmetrical form. One needs to wear certain spectacles, if one is to see everything at once. But you will notice that I repeat the eternal American tic of thinking about art in terms of its techniques. (This tic is shared by left wing and right wing and middle.) We talk about syllabics or sestinas or a colloquial vocabulary

* Frank O'Hara is included in the second edition.

or old spelling as if they made up a Little Marvel Poetry Kit, Free 10-Day Offer, One to a Customer, No Home Without It. The danger is that we may take technical variations more seriously than they warrant. We could argue that the movement which Robert Lowell typifies, from *Lord Weary's Castle* to *Life Studies*, is only a movement from one style of the twenties to another, from Allen Tate to William Carlos Williams, and that it is retrospective. If it makes it new, it makes it new within Lowell only.

One thing is happening in American poetry, as I see it, which is genuinely new. In lines like Robert Bly's:

> In small towns the houses are built right on the ground;
> The lamplight falls on all fours in the grass.

or Louis Simpson's:

> The clouds are lifting from the high Sierras,
> The Bay mists clearing;
> And the angel in the gate, the flowering plum,
> Dances like Italy, imagining red.

there is a kind of imagination new to American poetry. The vocabulary is mostly colloquial, but the special quality of the lines has nothing to do with an area of diction; it is a quality learned neither from T. S. Eliot nor William Carlos Williams. It is a quality closer to the spirit of Georg Trakl or Pablo Neruda, but it is not to be pigeon-holed according to any sources. This imagination is irrational, yet the poem is usually quiet and the language simple; there is no straining after apocalypse. There is an inwardness to these images, a profound subjectivity. Yet they are not subjective in the autobiographical manner of *Life Studies* or *Heart's Needle*, which are confessional and particular. Confessional poetry is certainly a widespread manner now in the United States. Snodgrass and Lowell were followed by Anne Sexton, and most effectively by Sylvia Plath in the remarkable poems she wrote before her death in 1963. Like any movement, confessional poetry has bred imitators swarming among the magazines. What began as a series of excruciating self-discoveries – often professionally aided by therapist or analyst – dissipates in an orgy of exhibitionism.

The movement which seems to me *new* is subjective but not autobiographical. It reveals through images not particular pain, but general subjective life. This universal subjective corresponds to the old objective life of shared experience and knowledge. People can talk to each other most deeply in images. To read a poem of this sort, you must not try to translate the images into abstractions. They won't go. You must try to be open to them, to let them take you over and speak in their own language of feeling. It is the intricate darkness of feeling and instinct which these poems mostly communicate. The poems are best described as expressionist: like the painter, the poet uses fantasy and distortion to express feeling. The poet may hesitate, when he is looking for a word, between opposites; would 'tiny' or 'huge' be better here?, 'mountain' or 'valley'? Such hesitation shows the irrationality and the arbitrariness of this method, but it does not imply that one of the alternatives is not enormously more appropriate than the other – only that neither is literal. The reader or the poet cannot go to the outside world and *check* – Ah, yes, the Empire State Building is 'huge' not 'tiny' – but we are not concerned with accuracy to externals; he can only make a subjective check with his inward world. When the painter hesitates between blue and green for the lady's face, he is at least certain that he will not paint it flesh-colour.

A word about making this anthology: I have made decisions about inclusions and exclusions which are highly arbitrary. I have included no poets who published books before *Lord Weary's Castle* in 1946, or who seemed to me to belong to an earlier period. The poets are arranged chronologically, *faute de mieux*; by a coincidence the oldest poet and the youngest published their first books within a year of each other.* I have included only poets of whom I could print several pages, because some variety of examples seems to me necessary in a book which acts as an introduction to new poets.

Ann Arbor, Michigan   DONALD HALL
1961; revised in 1963

POSTSCRIPT (1971)

Delay in printing this second edition has allowed me time for second thoughts.

When we decided to make a second edition, in 1966 I think, it was obvious that I could take one of two courses: I could add young poets (and supply others I had omitted through failure of taste); or I could expand and bring up to date the selections of the poets already included. The budget would not allow both.

I chose to add new poets. I even discarded a bit of the first edition to make more room. But now it is 1971, and poets of the 1962 edition are represented by early poems. Perhaps all of them – certainly Kinnell, Snyder, Bly, Hecht, Simpson, Rich – have written their best work in the last decade. I regret that this work is not here.

D. H.

* No longer true. (D. H., 1971).

PREFACE TO THE SECOND EDITION

MOST of the Introduction was written about eight years ago, in 1961. (I changed the conclusion in a reprinting; in the revision I mentioned the death of Sylvia Plath in 1963, but the date at the end of the Introduction remained 1961, which gave me the air of an awful prescience.) If I were writing the Introduction now, it would be different, and yet I do not find myself quarrelling with its general views of the history of recent American poetry. Perhaps my history is too tidy. But let it stand, and I will try to add to it, to expand it and to bring it up to date, as I have tried to do with my new selections, in the body of this revised anthology.

I suppose that 'the line of William Carlos Williams' has been more salient than any other line in the past decade. Old Objectivists have been dusted off and restored to the shelf where they always belonged; the names of Zukofsky and Rakosi, Oppen and Reznikoff, were heard again in the land – because of the predominance of a poetry resembling theirs, written by younger men.

Yet if a new orthodoxy begins to trouble American poetry now, it is not primarily an orthodoxy of Objectivism. It is a new convention, an orthodoxy of fantasy, of neo-surrealism, of the 'new imagination' – which in the first printing of this Introduction I said was 'so new that I lacked words for it'. (In the revised introduction I took to calling it 'expressionist'.) The poetry of Robert Bly, James Wright and Louis Simpson made my old examples. Now these poets have many followers, and there are other poets who resemble them simply because they derive their styles from the same sources. The youngest poets (centered geographically and spiritually in the East Village, with outposts on the West

Coast and everywhere else) are by no means followers of Bly and Wright, yet resemble them in significant ways. The youngest American poets (Benedikt, Clark and Padgett in this new edition) write a 'surrealism' which is harsher and has sharper edges than the fantastic meditations of the older poets. They are more French and less Spanish, more intellectually alert and less lyrical. Doubtless some members of the different generations despise each other's verse, but they resemble each other considerably more than any of them resemble, say, Howard Nemerov or Robert Creeley.

It does not matter. But probably fantastic poetry will become such a cliché – *bad* fantastic poetry – that it will be difficult to read the good things for a while. You can tell the dominance of a school by the prevalence of bad versions of it. Fifteen years ago, as I have said, it was bad Wilbur. Ten years ago it was bad *Life Studies*. Five years ago it was bad Robert Creeley. Now the magazines and publishers are overwhelmed by bad imitators of Pablo Neruda; everywhere the adjective 'dark' obscures soft nouns. (Robert Bly himself, in an article in *Kayak* criticizing past issues of *Kayak*, intelligently tried to be the dog that drowned his own fleas; but fleas are hard to kill.) The East Villagers, for whom John Ashbery and Frank O'Hara are the models, already have followers as large as a small anti-war army. The best of this poetry – these different poets, all irrational and fantastic, all devoted to the expressive image – is beautiful and strong. Long may it live, and death to the diluters.

IN making this new edition I have enlarged the book considerably, and changed its nature. In 1961 it was an interim report on fifteen years of post-war poetry. Now it attempts to contain nearly a quarter century of poetic experiment and achievement. It was a supplement before, and now it has become a thing in itself.

I have added Allen Ginsberg, whom it was ridiculous to

omit in the first place; I have added Sylvia Plath because her *Ariel* poems are now available – they were unwritten when I made the first collection; I have added David Ignatow whom I overlooked in 1961. Ignatow was born in 1914, and is the same age as the oldest poet in the original anthology, William Stafford. I have resisted the temptation to go back to earlier poets (Olson, Roethke) because I would not know where to stop. Having started arbitrarily with Stafford, I will use him as a time barrier. 1914 is also the birth-date of John Berryman whose *Dream Songs* I admire; he is not here because his publishers wished to charge a fee which it was impossible for Penguin Books to pay.

About schools, those boring and inevitable delineations: there are two more poets from the line of Williams: Dorn, Ammons; two confessional poets: Plath, Sexton; and a crowd of expressionists or neo-surrealists. There are also two black poets. A few years ago Karl Shapiro made some remarks about lily-white anthologies which made me angry, for the usual reason that one gets angry: because the remarks were accurate. A world of black poetry exists in America alongside the world of white poetry, exactly alike in structure – with its own publishers, bookstores, magazines, editors, anthologists, conferences, poetry readings – and almost entirely invisible to the white world. Like the rest of the black world. The world of white poetry has practised the usual genteel apartheid of tokenism: here is praise for Langston Hughes, here is a Pulitzer Prize for Gwendolyn Brooks; now we've done our liberal bit, let's go back to reading *The New York Review of Books*.

The world of black poetry seems to be thriving. I find it hard to judge these poems, as if I were trying to exercise my taste in a foreign language, which I am. Here I am printing two poets almost wholly unknown to the white world, Dudley Randall and Etheridge Knight. (I asked LeRoi Jones, who refused.) There are others I might have chosen, and the reader who is interested may look further in the

Journal of Black Poetry, Umbra, Soulbook, Black World and in the publications of the Broadside Press, for instance.

The poetry of the black American is not objectivist, surrealist or otherwise subject to labels. It is a poetry of reality, somewhat like the novelistic reality that Robert Lowell was after in *Life Studies*, but it is not confessional; there is nothing of the analyst's couch about it. It is a poetry of character, attending to qualities like courage, defiance and tenderness. I suspect that a great deal of the best American poetry of the last third of our century will be written by black Americans. 'All things fall and are built again/And those that build them again are gay.'

Ann Arbor, Michigan   DONALD HALL
1969

Travelling through the Dark

TRAVELLING through the dark I found a deer
dead on the edge of the Wilson River road.
It is usually best to roll them into the canyon:
that road is narrow; to swerve might make more dead.

By glow of the tail-light I stumbled back of the car
and stood by the heap, a doe, a recent killing;
she had stiffened already, almost cold.
I dragged her off; she was large in the belly.

My fingers touching her side brought me the reason –
her side was warm; her fawn lay there waiting,
alive, still, never to be born.
Beside that mountain road I hesitated.

The car aimed ahead its lowered parking lights;
under the hood purred the steady engine.
I stood in the glare of the warm exhaust turning red;
around our group I could hear the wilderness listen.

I thought hard for us all – my only swerving –
then pushed her over the edge into the river.

Returned to Say

WHEN I face north a lost Cree
on some new shore puts a moccasin down,
rock in the light and noon for seeing,
he in a hurry and I beside him.

It will be a long trip; he will be a new chief;
we have drunk new water from an unnamed stream;
under little dark trees he is to find a path
we both must travel because we have met.

Henceforth we gesture even by waiting;
there is a grain of sand on his knifeblade
so small he blows it and while his breathing
darkens the steel his eyes become set

And start a new vision: the rest of his life.
We will mean what he does. Back of this page
the path turns north. We are looking for a sign.
Our moccasins do not mark the ground.

At Cove on the Crooked River

At Cove at our camp in the open canyon
it was the kind of place where you might look out
some evening and see trouble walking away.

And the river there meant something
always coming from snow and flashing around boulders
after shadow-fish lurking below the mesa.

We stood with wet towels over our heads for shade,
looking past the Indian picture rock and the kind of trees
that act out whatever has happened to them.

Oh civilization, I want to carve you like this,
decisively outward the way evening comes
over that kind of twist in the scenery

When people cramp into their station wagons
and roll up the windows and drive away.

Strokes

THE left side of her world is gone –
the rest sustained by memory
and a realization: There are still the children.

Going down our porch steps her pastor
calls back: 'We are proud of her recovery,
and there is a chiropractor up in Galesburg . . .'

The birthdays of the old require such candles.

Near

TALKING along in this not quite prose way
we all know it is not quite prose we speak,
and it is time to notice this intolerable snow
innumerably touching, before we sink.

It is time to notice, I say, the freezing snow
hesitating toward us from others' grey heaven;
listen – it is falling not quite silently
and under it still you and I are walking.

Maybe there are trumpets in the houses we pass
and a redbird watching from an evergreen –
but nothing will happen until we pause
to flame what we know, before any signal's given.

With My Crowbar Key

I DO tricks in order to know:
careless I dance,
then turn to see
the mark to turn God left for me.

Making my home in vertigo
I pray with my screams
and think with my hair
prehensile in the dark with fear.

When I hear the well-bucket strike something soft
far down at noon,
then there's no place
far enough away to hide my face.

When I see my town over sights of a rifle,
and carved by light
from the lowering sun,
then my old friends darken one by one.

By step and step like a cat toward God
I dedicated walk,
but under the house
I realize the kitten's crouch.

And by night like this I turn and come
to this possible house
which I open, and see
myself at work with this crowbar key.

Roses and Revolutions

MUSING on roses and revolutions,
I saw night close down on the earth like a great dark wing,
and the lighted cities were like tapers in the night,
and I heard the lamentations of a million hearts
regretting life and crying for the grave,
and I saw the Negro lying in the swamp with his face blown
    off,
and in northern cities with his manhood maligned and felt
    the writhing
of his viscera like that of the hare hunted down or the bear
    at bay,
and I saw men working and taking no joy in their work
and embracing the hard-eyed whore with joyless excitement
and lying with wives and virgins in impotence.

And as I groped in darkness
and felt the pain of millions,
gradually, like day driving night across the continent,
I saw dawn upon them like the sun a vision
of a time when all men walk proudly through the earth
and the bombs and missiles lie at the bottom of the ocean
like the bones of dinosaurs buried under the shale of eras,
and men strive with each other not for power or the accu-
    mulation of paper
but in joy create for others the house, the poem, the game of
    athletic beauty.

Then washed in the brightness of this vision,
I saw how in its radiance would grow and be nourished and
    suddenly
burst into terrible and splendid bloom
the blood-red flower of revolution.

Black Poet, White Critic

A CRITIC advises
not to write on controversial subjects
like freedom or murder,
but to treat universal themes
and timeless symbols
like the white unicorn.

A *white* unicorn?

George

WHEN I was a boy desiring the title of man
And toiling to earn it
In the inferno of the foundry knockout,
I watched and admired you working by my side,
As, goggled, with mask on your mouth and shoulders bright
    with sweat,
You mastered the monstrous, lumpish cylinder blocks,
And when they clotted the line and plunged to the floor
With force enough to tear your foot in two,
You calmly stepped aside.

One day when the line broke down and the blocks clogged up
Groaning, grinding, and mounted like an ocean wave
And then rushed thundering down like an avalanche,
And we frantically dodged, then placed our heads together
To form an arch to lift and stack them,
You gave me your highest accolade:
You said, 'You're not afraid of sweat. You're strong as a
    mule.'

Now, here, in the hospital,
In a ward where old men wait to die,
You sit, and watch time go by.
You cannot read the books I bring, not even

Those that are only picture books,
As you sit among the senile wrecks,
The psychopaths, the incontinent.

One day when you fell from your chair and stared at the air
With the look of fright which sight of death inspires,
I lifted you like a cylinder block, and said,
'Don't be afraid
Of a little fall, for you'll be here
A long time yet, because you're strong as a mule.'

Old Witherington

OLD Witherington had drunk too much again.
The children changed their play and packed around him
To jeer his latest brawl. Their parents followed.

Prune-black, with bloodshot eyes and one white tooth.
He tottered in the night with legs spread wide
Waving a hatchet. 'Come on, come on,' he piped,
'And I'll baptize these bricks with bloody kindling.
I may be old and drunk, but not afraid
To die. I've died before. A million times
I've died and gone to hell. I live in hell.
If I die now I die, and put an end
To all this loneliness. Nobody cares
Enough to even fight me now, except
This crazy bastard here.'
                                    And with these words
He cursed the little children, cursed his neighbors,
Cursed his father, mother, and his wife,
Himself, and God, and all the rest of the world,
All but his grinning adversary, who, crouched,
Danced tenderly around him with a jag-toothed bottle,
As if the world compressed to one old man
Who was the sun, and he sole faithful planet.

The Bagel

I STOPPED to pick up the bagel
rolling away in the wind,
annoyed with myself
for having dropped it
as it were a portent.
Faster and faster it rolled,
with me running after it
bent low, gritting my teeth,
and I found myself doubled over
and rolling down the street
head over heels, one complete somersault
after another like a bagel
and strangely happy with myself.

Rescue the Dead

FINALLY, to forgo love is to kiss a leaf,
is to let rain fall nakedly upon your head,
is to respect fire,
is to study man's eyes and his gestures
as he talks,
is to set bread upon the table
and a knife discreetly by,
is to pass through crowds
like a crowd of oneself.
Not to love is to live.

To love is to be led away
into a forest where the secret grave
is dug, singing, praising darkness
under the trees.

46

To live is to sign your name,
is to ignore the dead,
is to carry a wallet
and shake hands.

To love is to be a fish.
My boat wallows in the sea.
You who are free,
rescue the dead.

Ritual Three

In England, the slow methodical torture of two children
was recorded on tape by the murderers.

I

It's quiet for me, now that I have buried the child.
I am resting, rid of a menace to my peace,
since I am not here for long either.
What she said was that she wanted to go back
to her mother, so help her God, and I believed her,
and they did too who cut her slowly into flesh,
but it was another mother they had in mind.
Let me rest, let me rest from their mistakes.
They were human like myself, somehow
gone in a direction to a depth I've never known.
I am not thinking,
I am contemptuous of thought.
I growl in my depths, I find blood flowing
across my tongue and enjoy its taste.
Call me man, I don't care.
I am content with myself,
I have a brain that gives me the pleasure.
Come here and I will tear you to pieces,
it'll be catch as catch can
but I can throw you who are weakened with the horror
of what I say, so surrender peacefully

and let me take my first bite directly above your heart.
I am a man, your life lost in feeling,
I never knew what mercy meant,
I am free.

II

Child gone to a calm grave,
I want to be a crocodile,
opening the two blades of my mouth.
I'll slide through swamp, taking in small fish and flies.
I will not run a knife across the skin
or cut off a nose or tear off the genitals,
as screams fade in exhaustion.
Nobody could force me, as I threaten with my jaws,
safe for a moment as I dream I am sane, purposeful
and on my course, dreaming that we no longer should trouble
to live as human beings, that we should discuss this,
putting aside our wives and children,
for to live is to act in terms of death.

East Bronx

In the street two children sharpen
knives against the curb.
Parents leaning out the window
above gaze and think and smoke
and duck back into the house
to sit on the toilet seat
with locked door to read
of the happiness of two tortoises
on an island in the Pacific —
always alone and always
the sun shining.

All Quiet

(For Robert Bly)
Written at the start of one of our bombing pauses
over North Vietnam.

How come nobody is being bombed today?
I want to know, being a citizen
of this country and a family man.
You can't take my fate in your hands,
without informing me.
I can blow up a bomb or crush a skull —
whoever started this peace
without advising me
through a news leak
at which I could have voiced a protest,
running my whole family off a cliff.

Christmas Eve under Hooker's Statue

TONIGHT a blackout. Twenty years ago
I hung my stocking on the tree, and hell's
Serpent entwined the apple in the toe
To sting the child with knowledge. Hooker's heels
Kicking at nothing in the shifting snow,
A cannon and a cairn of cannon balls
Rusting before the blackened Statehouse, know
How the long horn of plenty broke like glass
In Hooker's gauntlets. Once I came from Mass;

Now storm-clouds shelter Christmas, once again
Mars meets his fruitless star with open arms,
His heavy sabre flashes with the rime,
The war-god's bronzed and empty forehead forms
Anonymous machinery from raw men;
The cannon on the Common cannot stun
The blundering butcher as he rides on Time —
The barrel clinks with holly. I am cold:
I ask for bread, my father gives me mould;

His stocking is full of stones. Santa in red
Is crowned with wizened berries. Man of war,
Where is the summer's garden? In its bed
The ancient speckled serpent will appear,
And black-eyed Susan with her frizzled head.
When Chancellorsville mowed down the volunteer,
'All wars are boyish,' Herman Melville said;
But we are old, our fields are running wild:
Till Christ again turn wanderer and child.

The Holy Innocents

LISTEN, the hay-bells tinkle as the cart
Wavers on rubber tyres along the tar
And cindered ice below the burlap mill
And ale-wife run. The oxen drool and start
In wonder at the fenders of a car,
And blunder hugely up St Peter's hill.
These are the undefiled by woman – their
Sorrow is not the sorrow of this world:
King Herod shrieking vengeance at the curled-
Up knees of Jesus choking in the air,

A king of speechless clods and infants. Still
The world out-Herods Herod; and the year,
The nineteen-hundred forty-fifth of grace,
Lumbers with losses up the clinkered hill
Of our purgation; and the oxen near
The worn foundations of their resting-place,
The holy manger where their bed is corn
And holly torn for Christmas. If they die,
As Jesus, in the harness, who will mourn?
Lamb of the shepherds, Child, how still you lie.

New Year's Day

AGAIN and then again ... the year is born
To ice and death, and it will never do
To skulk behind storm-windows by the stove
To hear the postgirl sounding her French horn
When the thin tidal ice is wearing through.
Here is the understanding not to love
Each other, or tomorrow that will sieve
Our resolutions. While we live, we live

To snuff the smoke of victims. In the snow
The kitten heaved its hindlegs, as if fouled,
And died. We bent it in a Christmas box
And scattered blazing weeds to scare the crow
Until the snake-tailed sea-winds coughed and howled
For alms outside the church whose double locks
Wait for St Peter, the distorted key.
Under St Peter's bell the parish sea

Swells with its smelt into the burlap shack
Where Joseph plucks his hand-lines like a harp,
And hears the fearful *Puer natus est*
Of Circumcision, and relives the wrack
And howls of Jesus whom he holds. How sharp
The burden of the Law before the beast:
Time and the grindstone and the knife of God.
The Child is born in blood, O child of blood.

Katherine's Dream

From *Between the Porch and the Altar*

It must have been a Friday. I could hear
The top-floor typist's thunder and the beer
That you had brought in cases hurt my head;
I'd sent the pillows flying from my bed,
I hugged my knees together and I gasped.
The dangling telephone receiver rasped
Like someone in a dream who cannot stop
For breath or logic till his victim drop
To darkness and the sheets. I must have slept,
But still could hear my father who had kept
Your guilty presents but cut off my hair.
He whispers that he really doesn't care
If I am your kept woman all my life,
Or ruin your two children and your wife;

But my dishonour makes him drink. Of course
I'll tell the court the truth for his divorce.
I walk through snow into St Patrick's yard.
Black nuns with glasses smile and stand on guard
Before a bulkhead in a bank of snow,
Whose charred doors open, as good people go
Inside by twos to the confessor. One
Must have a friend to enter there, but none
Is friendless in this crowd, and the nuns smile.
I stand aside and marvel; for a while
The winter sun is pleasant and it warms
My heart with love for others, but the swarms
Of penitents have dwindled. I begin
To cry and ask God's pardon of our sin.
Where are you? You were with me and are gone.
All the forgiven couples hurry on
To dinner and their nights, and none will stop.
I run about in circles till I drop
Against a padlocked bulkhead in a yard
Where faces redden and the snow is hard.

After the Surprising Conversions

SEPTEMBER twenty-second, Sir: today
I answer. In the latter part of May,
Hard on our Lord's Ascension, it began
To be more sensible. A gentleman
Of more than common understanding, strict
In morals, pious in behaviour, kicked
Against our goad. A man of some renown,
An useful, honoured person in the town,
He came of melancholy parents; prone
To secret spells, for years they kept alone —

His uncle, I believe, was killed of it:
Good people, but of too much or little wit.
I preached one Sabbath on a text from Kings;
He showed concernment for his soul. Some things
In his experience were hopeful. He
Would sit and watch the wind knocking a tree
And praise this countryside our Lord has made.
Once when a poor man's heifer died, he laid
A shilling on the doorsill; though a thirst
For loving shook him like a snake, he durst
Not entertain much hope of his estate
In heaven. Once we saw him sitting late
Behind his attic window by a light
That guttered on his Bible; through that night
He meditated terror, and he seemed
Beyond advice or reason, for he dreamed
That he was called to trumpet Judgement Day
To Concord. In the latter part of May
He cut his throat. And though the coroner
Judged him delirious, soon a noisome stir
Palsied our village. At Jehovah's nod
Satan seemed more let loose amongst us: God
Abandoned us to Satan, and he pressed
Us hard, until we thought we could not rest
Till we had done with life. Content was gone.
All the good work was quashed. We were undone.
The breath of God had carried out a planned
And sensible withdrawal from this land;
The multitude, once unconcerned with doubt,
Once neither callous, curious, nor devout,
Jumped at broad noon, as though some peddler groaned
At it in its familiar twang: 'My friend,
Cut your own throat. Cut your own throat. Now! Now!'
September twenty-second, Sir, the bough
Cracks with the unpicked apples, and at dawn
The small-mouth bass breaks water, gorged with spawn.

Memories of West Street and Lepke

ONLY teaching on Tuesdays, book-worming
in pyjamas fresh from the washer each morning,
I hog a whole house on Boston's
'hardly passionate Marlborough Street',
where even the man
scavenging filth in the back alley trash cans,
has two children, a beach wagon, a helpmate,
and is a 'young Republican'.
I have a nine months' daughter,
young enough to be my granddaughter.
Like the sun she rises in her flame-flamingo infants' wear.

These are the tranquillized *Fifties*,
and I am forty. Ought I to regret my seedtime?
I was a fire-breathing Catholic C.O.,
and made my manic statement,
telling off the state and president, and then
sat waiting sentence in the bull pen
beside a Negro boy with curlicues
of marijuana in his hair.

Given a year,
I walked on the roof of the West Street Jail, a short
enclosure like my school soccer court,
and saw the Hudson River once a day
through sooty clothesline entanglements
and bleaching khaki tenements.
Strolling, I yammered metaphysics with Abramowitz,
a jaundice-yellow ('it's really tan')
and fly-weight pacifist,
so vegetarian,
he wore rope shoes and preferred fallen fruit.
He tried to convert Bioff and Brown,
the Hollywood pimps, to his diet.

Hairy, muscular, suburban,
wearing chocolate double-breasted suits,
they blew their tops and beat him black and blue.

I was so out of things, I'd never heard
of the Jehovah's Witnesses.
'Are you a C. O.?' I asked a fellow jailbird.
'No,' he answered, 'I'm a J. W.'
He taught me the 'hospital tuck',
and pointed out the T-shirted back
of *Murder Incorporated*'s Czar Lepke,
there piling towels on a rack,
or dawdling off to his little segregated cell full
of things forbidden the common man:
a portable radio, a dresser, two toy American
flags tied together with a ribbon of Easter palm.
Flabby, bald, lobotomized,
he drifted in a sheepish calm,
where no agonizing reappraisal
jarred his concentration on the electric chair –
hanging like an oasis in his air
of lost connexions. . . .

For Sale

POOR sheepish plaything,
organized with prodigal animosity,
lived in just a year –
my Father's cottage at Beverly Farms
was on the market the month he died.
Empty, open, intimate,
its town-house furniture
had an on tiptoe air
of waiting for the mover
on the heels of the undertaker.

Ready, afraid
of living alone till eighty,
Mother mooned in a window,
as if she had stayed on a train
one stop past her destination.

Man and Wife

TAMED by *Miltown*, we lie on Mother's bed;
the rising sun in war paint dyes us red;
in broad daylight her gilded bed-posts shine,
abandoned, almost Dionysian.
At last the trees are green on Marlborough Street,
blossoms on our magnolia ignite
the morning with their murderous five days' white.
All night I've held your hand,
as if you had
a fourth time faced the kingdom of the mad –
its hackneyed speech, its homicidal eye –
and dragged me home alive. . . . Oh my *Petite*,
clearest of all God's creatures, still all air and nerve:
you were in your twenties, and I,
once hand on glass
and heart in mouth,
outdrank the Rahvs in the heat
of Greenwich Village, fainting at your feet –
too boiled and shy
and poker-faced to make a pass,
while the shrill verve
of your invective scorched the traditional South.

Now, twelve years later, you turn your back.
Sleepless, you hold
your pillow to your hollows like a child;
your old-fashioned tirade –
loving, rapid, merciless –
breaks like the Atlantic Ocean on my head.

Skunk Hour
(For Elizabeth Bishop)

NAUTILUS Island's hermit
heiress still lives through winter in her Spartan cottage;
her sheep still graze above the sea.
Her son's a bishop. Her farmer
is first selectman in our village;
she's in her dotage.

Thirsting for
the hierarchic privacy
of Queen Victoria's century,
she buys up all
the eyesores facing her shore,
and lets them fall.

The season's ill –
we've lost our summer millionaire,
who seemed to leap from an L. L. Bean
catalogue. His nine-knot yawl
was auctioned off to lobstermen.
A red fox stain covers Blue Hill.

And now our fairy
decorator brightens his shop for fall;
his fishnet's filled with orange cork,
orange, his cobbler's bench and awl;
there is no money in his work,
he'd rather marry.

One dark night,
my Tudor Ford climbed the hill's skull;
I watched for love-cars. Lights turned down,
they lay together, hull to hull,
where the graveyard shelves on the town. . . .
My mind's not right.

A car radio bleats,
'Love, O careless Love. . . .' I hear
my ill-spirit sob in each blood cell,
as if my hand were at its throat. . . .
I myself am hell;
nobody's here –

only skunks, that search
in the moonlight for a bite to eat.
They march on their soles up Main Street:
white stripes, moonstruck eyes' red fire
under the chalk-dry and spar spire
of the Trinitarian Church.

I stand on top
of our back steps and breathe the rich air –
a mother skunk with her column of kittens swills the garbage
    pail.
She jabs her wedge-head in a cup
of sour cream, drops her ostrich tail,
and will not scare.

A Poem Beginning with a Line by Pindar

I

THE light foot hears you and the brightness begins
god-step at the margins of thought,
    quick adulterous tread at the heart.
Who is it that goes there?
    Where I see your quick face
notes of an old music pace the air
torso-reverberations of a Grecian lyre.

In Goya's canvas Cupid and Psyche
have a hurt voluptuous grace
bruised by redemption. The copper light
falling upon the brown boy's slight body
is carnal fate that sends the soul wailing
up from blind innocence, ensnared
    by dimness
into the deprivations of desiring sight.

But the eyes in Goya's painting are soft,
diffuse with rapture absorb the flame.
Their bodies yield out of strength.
    Waves of visual pleasure
wrap them in a sorrow previous to their impatience.

A bronze of yearning, a rose that burns
    the tips of their bodies, lips,
ends of fingers, nipples. He is not wingd.
His thighs are flesh, are clouds
    lit by the sun in its going down,
hot luminescence at the loins of the visible.

But they are not in a landscape.
They exist in an obscurity.

The wind spreading the sail serves them.
The two jealous sisters eager for her ruin
    serve them.
That she is ignorant, ignorant of what Love will be,
    serves them,
The dark serves them.
The oil scalding his shoulder serves them,
serves their story. Fate, spinning,
    knots the threads for Love.

Jealousy, ignorance, the hurt . . . serve them.

II

This is magic. It is passionate dispersion.
What if they grow old? The gods
    would not allow it.
    Psyche is preserved.

In time we see a tragedy, a loss of beauty
    the glittering youth
of the god retains – but from this threshold
    it is age
that is beautiful. It is toward the old poets
    we go, to their faltering,
their unaltering wrongness that has style,
    their variable truth,
    the old faces,
words shed like tears from
a plenitude of powers time stores.

A stroke.   These little strokes.   A chill.
    The old man, feeble, does not recoil.
Recall. A phase so minute,
    only a part of the word in-jerrd.

The Thundermakers descend,

damerging a nuv. A nerb.
　　The present dented of the U
nighted stayd.　States.　The heavy clod?
　　Cloud.　Invades the brain.　What
　　if lilacs last in *this* dooryard bloomd?

Hoover, Roosevelt, Truman, Eisenhower—
where among these did the power reside
that moves the heart? What flower of the nation
bride-sweet broke to the whole rapture?
Hoover, Coolidge, Harding, Wilson,
hear the factories of human misery turning out commodities.
For whom are the holy matins of the heart ringing?
Noble men in the quiet of morning hear
Indians singing the continent's violent requiem.
Harding, Wilson, Taft, Roosevelt,
idiots fumbling at the bride's door,
hear the cries of men in meaningless debt and war.
Where among these did the spirit reside
that restores the land to productive order?
McKinley, Cleveland, Harrison, Arthur,
Garfield, Hayes, Grant, Johnson,
dwell in the roots of the heart's rancour.
How sad 'amid lanes and through old woods'
　　echoes Whitman's love for Lincoln!

There is no continuity then.　Only a few
　　posts of the good remain.　I too
that am a nation sustain the damage
　　where smokes of continual ravage
obscure the flame.
　　　　　　　　It is across great scars of wrong
　　I reach toward the song of kindred men
　　and strike again the naked string
old Whitman sang from.　Glorious mistake!
　　that cried:

'The theme is creative and has vista.'
'He is the president of regulation.'

    I see always the under-side turning,
  fumes that injure the tender landscape.
    From which up break
lilac blossoms of courage in daily act
      striving to meet a natural measure.

III

(*for Charles Olson*)

        Psyche's tasks – the sorting of seeds
wheat   barley   oats   poppy   coriander
anise   beans   lentils   peas – every grain
        in its right place
            before nightfall;

gathering the gold wool from the cannibal sheep
(for the soul must weep
  and come near upon death);

harrowing Hell for a casket Proserpina keeps
             that must not
  be opend . . . containing beauty?

no! Melancholy coild like a serpent
           that is deadly sleep
  we are not permitted
        to succumb to.

  These are the old tasks.
  You've heard them before.

  They must be impossible. Psyche
must despair, be brought to her
          insect instructor;

must obey the counsels of the green reed;
saved from suicide by a tower speaking,
   must follow to the letter
   freakish instructions.

In the story the ants help. The old man at Pisa
   mixd in whose mind
(to draw the sorts) are all seeds
      as a lone ant from a broken ant-hill
had part restored by an insect, was
   upheld by a lizard

            (to draw the sorts)
the wind is part of the process
            defines a nation of the wind –
   father of many notions,

              Who?
let the light into the dark? began
the many movements of the passion?

                West
from east   men push.
           The islands are blessd
(cursed)   that swim below the sun,

   man upon whom the sun has gone down!

There is the hero who struggles east
widdershins to free the dawn   and must
            woo Night's daughter,
sorcery, black passionate rage, covetous queens,
so that the fleecy sun go   back from Troy,
   Colchis, India . . . all the blazing armies
spent, he must struggle alone toward the pyres of Day.

          The light that is Love
rushes on toward passion.   It verges upon dark.
   Roses and blood flood the clouds.
   Solitary first riders advance into legend.

This land, where I stand, was all legend
in my grandfathers' time: cattle raiders,
    animal tribes, priests, gold.
It was the West. Its vistas painters saw
    in diffuse light, in melancholy,
in abysses left by glaciers as if they had been the sun
    primordial carving empty enormities
                    out of the rock.

                    Snakes lurkd
guarding secrets.   Those first ones
                    survived solitude.

    Scientia
holding the lamp, driven by doubt;
Eros naked in foreknowledge
smiling in his sleep;   and the light
spilld, burning his shoulder – the outrage
    that conquers legend –
passion, dismay, longing, search
    flooding up where
the Beloved is lost.   Psyche travels
life after life, my life, station
    after station,
to be tried

    without break, without
news, knowing only – but what did she know?
    The oracle at Miletus had spoken
truth surely: that he was Serpent-Desire
    that flies thru the air,
a monster-husband. But she saw him fair

whom Apollo's mouthpiece said spread
    pain
beyond cure   to those
    wounded by his arrows.

Rilke torn by a rose thorn
blackend toward Eros.   Cupidinous Death!
　　that will not take no for an answer.

IV

　　Oh yes!   Bless the footfall where
step by step   the boundary walker
(in Maverick Road   the snow
thud by thud   from the roof
circling the house – another tread)

　　that foot   informd
by the weight of all things
　　that can be elusive
no more than a nearness to the mind
　　of a single image

　　　　Oh yes!   this
most dear
　　the catalyst force that renders clear
the days of a life from the surrounding medium!

　　　　Yes, beautiful rare wilderness!
wildness that verifies strength of my tame mind,
　　clearing held against indians,
health that prepared to meet death,
　　the stubborn hymns going up
into the ramifications of the hostile air

　　that, deceptive, gives way.

Who is there?   O, light the light!
　　The Indians give way,   the clearing falls.
Great Death gives way   and unprepares us.
　　Lust gives way.   The Moon gives way.
Night gives way.   Minutely,   the Day gains.

She saw the body of her beloved
   dismemberd in waking ... or was it
in sight? *Finders Keepers* we sang
   when we were children   or were taught to sing
before our histories began   and we began
   who were beloved   our animal life
toward the Beloved,   sworn to be Keepers.

   On the hill before the wind came
the grass moved toward the one sea,
   blade after blade dancing in waves.

There the children turn the ring to the left.
There the children turn the ring to the right.
   Dancing ... Dancing ...

And the lonely psyche goes up thru the boy to the king
   that in the caves of history dreams.
Round and round the children turn.
   London Bridge that is a kingdom falls.

We have come so far that all the old stories
whisper once more.
Mount Segur, Mount Victoire, Mount Tamalpais ...
   rise to adore the mystery of Love!

(An ode? Pindar's art, the editors tell us, was not a statue but
a mosaic, an accumulation of metaphor. But if he was archaic,
not classic, a survival of obsolete mode, there may have been
old voices in the survival that directed the heart. So, a line
from a hymn came in a novel I was reading to help me.
Psyche, poised to leap – and Pindar too, the editors write,
goes too far, topples over – listend to a tower that said
Listen to me! The oracle had said, *Despair! The Gods them-
selves abhor his power.* And then the virgin flower of the dark
falls back flesh of our flesh from which everywhere ...)

the information flows
 that is yearning. A line of Pindar
moves from the area of my lamp
 toward morning.

In the dawn that is nowhere
 I have seen the wilful children

clockwise and counter-clockwise turning.

Still Life

I MUST explain why it is that at night, in my own house,
Even when no one's asleep, I feel I must whisper.
Thoreau and Wordsworth would call it an act of devotion,
I think; others would call it fright; it is probably
Something of both. In my living-room there are matters I'd
    rather not meddle with
Late at night.

I prefer to sit very still on the couch, watching
All the inanimate things of my daytime life –
The furniture and the curtains, the pictures and books –
Come alive,
Not as in some childish fantasy, the chairs dancing
And Disney prancing backstage, but with dignity,
The big old rocker presiding over a silent
And solemn assembly of all my craftsmen,
From Picasso and other dignities gracing my walls
To the local carpenter benched at my slippered feet.

I find these proceedings
Remarkable for their clarity and intelligence, and I wish I
    might somehow
Bring into daylight the eloquence, say, of a doorknob.
But always the gathering breaks up; everyone there
Shrinks from the tossing turbulence
Of living,
A cough, a creaking stair.

A Day with the Foreign Legion

ON one of those days with the Legion
When everyone sticks to sofas
And itches and bitches – a day
For gin and bitters and the plague –
Down by Mount Tessala, under the plane trees,
Seated at iron tables, cursing the country,
Cursing the times and the natives, cursing the drinks,
Cursing the food and the bugs, cursing the Legion,
Were Kim and Bim and all those brave
Heroes of all those books and plays and movies
The remorseless desert serves.
And as they sat at the iron tables cursing the country,
Cursing the food and the bugs, cursing the Legion,
Some Sergeant or other rushed in from The Fort
Gallantly bearing the news
From which all those the remorseless desert serves
Take their cues:
'Sir!'
          'What is it, Sergeant?'
                              'Sir, the hordes
March e'en now across the desert swards.'

Just like the movies.

Now in the movies
The Sergeant's arrival touches off bugles and bells,
Emptying bunks and showers, frightening horses,
Pushing up flags and standards, hardening lines
Of unsoldierly softness, and putting farewells
Hastily in the post so two weeks hence
A perfectly lovely lovely in far-off Canada
Will go pale and bite buttons and stare at the air in Canada.
And in the movies,
Almost before the audience spills its popcorn,

The company's formed and away, with Bim or Kim
Solemnly leading them out into a sandstorm,
Getting them into what is quite clearly a trap,
Posting a double guard,
Sending messengers frantic to Marrakech,
Inadvertently pouring the water away,
Losing the ammunition, horses and food,
And generally carrying on in the great tradition
By making speeches
Which bring back to mind the glorious name of the Legion,
And serve as the turning point,
After which the Arabs seem doped and perfectly helpless,
Water springs up from the ground, the horses come back,
Plenty of food is discovered in some old cave,
And reinforcements arrive led by the girl
From Canada.

But in this instance nothing from *Beau Geste*
Or the Paramount lot was attempted,
It being too hot, too terribly hot, for dramatics
Even from Kim and Bim
Aging under the plane trees,
Cursing the food and the bugs, cursing the Sergeant
Who gallantly bore the news because he was young,
Full of oats and ignorance, so damned young
In his pretty khaki; nothing at all,
So late in the day, with everyone crocked
And bitten to death and sweaty and all,
Was attempted despite the Sergeant,
Who whirled on his heel, his mission accomplished, and
    marched,
Hip hip,
Out of the bar, a true trooper, as if to the wars.

So the lights went on and the audience,
Pleasantly stupid, whistled and clapped at the rarity
Of a film breaking down in this late year of Our Lord.

But of course it was not the film; it was not the projector;
Nor was it the man in the booth, who hastened away
As soon as the feature was over, leaving the heroes
Cursing the food and the bugs, cursing the Legion
As heathendom marched and the Sergeant whirled, hip hip;
But some other, darker cause having to do
With the script perhaps, or the art.
Or not art —
None of these but still deeper, deeper and darker,
Rooted in Culture or . . . Culture, or . . .

Or none of these things. Or all.

What was it?

None of these things, or all. It was the time,
The time and the place, and how could one blame them,
Seated at iron tables cursing the country?
What could they do,
Seated under the plane trees watching the Sergeant
Whirl on his heel, hip hip, in his pretty khaki?
What could they say,
Drinking their gin and bitters by Mount Tessala,
What could they say?

For what after all *could* be said,
After all was said,
But that the feature had merely run out, and the lights had
    gone on
Because it was time for the lights to go on, and time
For them not to dash out in the desert,
But to rage
As befitted their age
At the drinks and the country, letting their audience
Clap, stamp, whistle and hoot as darkness
Settled on Mount Tessala, the lights went on,
The enemy roamed the desert, and everyone itched.

On the Suicide of a Friend

SOME there are who are present at such occasions,
And conduct themselves with appropriate feeling and grace.
But they are the rare ones. Mostly the friends and relations
Are caught playing cards or eating miles from the place.
What happens on that dark river, or road, or mountain
Passes unnoticed as friend trumps loved one's ace.
Perhaps he knew this about them – worse, he did not,
And raged over the brink of that road or mountain
Thinking at least they'd remember before they forgot.
Either way, now he is dead and done with that lot.

The Party

THEY served tea in the sandpile, together with
Mudpies baked on the sidewalk.
After tea
The youngest said that he had had a good dinner,
The oldest dressed for a dance,
And they sallied forth together with watering pots
To moisten a rusted fire truck on account of it
Might rain.

I watched from my study,
Thought of my part in these contributions to world
Gaiety, and resolved
That the very least acknowledgement I could make
Would be to join them;
                              so we
All took our watering pots (filled with pies)
And poured tea on our dog. Then I kissed the children
And told them that when they grew up we would have
Real tea parties.
'That did be fun!' the youngest shouted, and ate pies
With wild surmise.

The Walk Home

As one grows older and Caesar, Hitler,
Lear, and the salesman are bundled off one by one,
It is hard to sustain discomposure. The files thicken.
'Leaves,' says the poet, 'grass, and birds of the field,'
Conjuring up a glass and a good book
On some green hill
Where nobody bears or cares more than old care will.

Who's in, who's out – such words harden
In bronze or plastic; pipes and slippers
Move to their destined places, swords to theirs;
And one walking home at dusk with the evening paper
Thinks with erosive irreverence that perhaps
He should let his subscription to that sheet lapse.

What, then, would the world do? As swords clashed
Under the sun, and Prince Hal and Sir Winston
Triumphed on all continents, would then the word
Sweep the ranks that one watching watched no longer?
As he closed his eyes to all but his own thin theme,
Would the world then oblige, age and dream his dream?

Dream. Dream. And still dream. And leave not a wrack.
As one grows older
Plato's, Bottom's and all such country rouses
Thicken the files with the rest;
And walking home at dusk with the sages, age
Thinks no more than age must always think:–
The world doesn't oblige, and old pipes stink.

Storm Windows

PEOPLE are putting up storm windows now,
Or were, this morning, until the heavy rain
Drove them indoors. So, coming home at noon,
I saw storm windows lying on the ground,
Frame-full of rain; through the water and glass
I saw the crushed grass, how it seemed to stream
Away in lines like seaweed on the tide
Or blades of wheat leaning under the wind.
The ripple and splash of rain on the blurred glass
Seemed that it briefly said, as I walked by,
Something I should have liked to say to you,
Something . . . the dry grass bent under the pane
Brimful of bouncing water . . . something of
A swaying clarity which blindly echoes
This lonely afternoon of memories
And missed desires, while the wintry rain
(Unspeakable, the distance in the mind!)
Runs on the standing windows and away.

The Statues in the Public Gardens

ALONE at the end of green *allées*, alone
Where a path turns back upon itself, or else
Where several paths converge, green bronze, grey stone,
The weatherbeaten famous figures wait
Inside their basins, on their pedestals,
Till time, as promised them, wears out of date.

Around them rise the willow, birch, and elm,
Sweet shaken pliancies in the weather now.

75

The granite hand is steady on the helm,
The sword, the pen, unshaken in the hand,
The bandage and the laurel on the brow:
The last obedience is the last command.

Children and nurses eddying through the day,
Old gentlemen with newspapers and canes,
And licit lovers, public as a play,
Never acknowledge the high regard of fame
Across their heads – the patriot's glare, the pains
Of prose – and scarcely stop to read a name.

Children, to be illustrious is sad.
Do not look up. Those empty eyes are stars,
Their glance the constellation of the mad
Who must be turned to stone. To save your garden,
My playful ones, these pallid voyagers
Stand in the streak of rain, imploring pardon.

At night the other lovers come to play
Endangered games, and robbers lie in wait
To knock old ladies with a rock; but they
Tremble to come upon these stony men
And suffragettes, who shine like final fate
In the electric green of every glen.

For it is then that statues suffer their
Sacrificed lives, and sigh through fruitless trees
After the flesh. Their sighs tremble the air,
They would surrender sceptres, swords, and globes,
Feeling the soft flank shudder to the breeze
Under the greatcoats and the noble robes.

In darker glades, the nearly naked stone
Of athlete, goddess chaste as any snows
That stain them winters, tempts maiden and man
From their prosthetic immortality:
Pythagoras' thigh, or Tycho's golden nose,
For a figleaf fallen from the withered tree.

A Singular Metamorphosis

WE all were watching the quiz on television
Last night, combining leisure with pleasure,
When Uncle Henry's antique *escritoire*,
Where he used to sit making up his accounts,
Began to shudder and rock like a crying woman,
Then burst into flower from every cubbyhole
(For all the world like a seventy-four of the line
Riding the swell and firing off Finisterre).
Extraordinary sight! Its delicate legs
Thickened and gnarled, writhing, they started to root
The feet deep in a carpet of briony
Star-pointed with primula. Small animals
Began to mooch around and climb up this
Reversionary desk and dustable heirloom
Left in the gloomiest corner of the room
Far from the television.
                                        I alone,
To my belief, remarked the remarkable
Transaction above remarked. The flowers were blue,
The fiery blue of iris, and there was
A smell of warm, wet grass and new horse-dung.

The screen, meanwhile, communicated to us
With some fidelity the image and voice
Of Narcisse, the cultivated policewoman
From San Francisco, who had already
Taken the sponsors for ten thousand greens
By knowing her Montalets from Capegues,
Cordilleras from Gonorrheas, in
The Plays of Shapesmoke Swoon of Avalon,
A tygers hart in a players painted hide
If ever you saw one.
                                When all this was over,
And everyone went home to bed, not one

77

Mentioned the *escritoire*, which was by now
Bowed over with a weight of fruit and nuts
And birds and squirrels in its upper limbs.
Stars tangled with its mistletoe and ivy.

The View from an Attic Window
(For Francis and Barbara)

I

AMONG the high-branching, leafless boughs
Above the roof-peaks of the town,
Snowflakes unnumberably come down.

I watched out of the attic window
The laced sway of family trees,
Intricate genealogies

Whose strict, reserved gentility,
Trembling, impossible to bow,
Received the appalling fall of snow.

All during Sunday afternoon,
Not storming, but befittingly,
Out of a still, grey, devout sky,

The snowflakes fell, until all shapes
Went under, and thickening, drunken lines
Cobwebbed the sleep of solemn pines.

Up in the attic, among many things
Inherited and out of style,
I cried, then fell asleep awhile,

Waking at night now, as the snow-
flakes from darkness to darkness go
Past yellow lights in the street below.

II

I cried because life is hopeless and beautiful.
And like a child I cried myself to sleep
High in the head of the house, feeling the hull
Beneath me pitch and roll among the steep
Mountains and valleys of the many years
   Which brought me to tears.

Down in the cellar, furnace and washing machine,
Pump, fuse-box, water-heater, work their hearts
Out at my life, which narrowly runs between
Them and this cemetery of spare parts
For discontinued men, whose hats and canes
   Are my rich remains.

And women, their portraits and wedding gowns
Stacked in the corners, brooding in wooden trunks;
And children's rattles, books about lions and clowns;
And headless, hanging dresses sway like drunks
Whenever a living footstep shakes the floor;
   I mention no more;

But what I thought today, that made me cry,
Is this, that we live in two kinds of thing:
The powerful trees, thrusting into the sky
Their black patience, are one, and that branching
Relation teaches how we endure and grow;
   The other is the snow,

Falling in a white chaos from the sky,
As many as the sands of all the seas,
As all the men who died or who will die,
As stars in heaven, as leaves of all the trees;
As Abraham was promised of his seed;
   Generations bleed,

Till I, high in the tower of my time
Among familiar ruins, began to cry
For accident, sickness, justice, war and crime,
Because all died, because I had to die.
The snow fell, the trees stood, the promise kept,
  And a child I slept.

The Fall Again

It is the Old Man through the sleeping town
Comes oil-dark to a certain lip, and breaks
By the white rain's beard the word he speaks,
A drunken Babel that stuns on a stone
And leaps in shatterings of light against
Its pouring fall, and falls again to spill
Asleep its darkening strength along the kill
On those great sinews' curves twisted and tensed.
Between the vineyard and the drunken dark,
O sorrow, there the rainbow shines no more,
There promises are broken in the roar
Of that Old Man, the staggered Patriarch
And whitebeard falling naked to the floor
Ashamed, who was himself both Flood and Ark.

Tywater

DEATH of Sir Nihil, book the nth,
Upon the charred and clotted sward,
Lacking the lily of our Lord,
Alases of the hyacinth.

Could flicker from behind his ear
A whistling silver throwing knife
And with a holler punch the life
Out of a swallow in the air.

Behind the lariat's butterfly
Shuttled his white and gritted grin,
And cuts of sky would roll within
The noose-hole, when he spun it high.

The violent, neat and practised skill
Was all he loved and all he learned;
When he was hit, his body turned
To clumsy dirt before it fell.

And what to say of him, God knows.
Such violence. And such repose.

'*A World Without Objects is a Sensible Emptiness*'

THE tall camels of the spirit
Steer for their deserts, passing the last groves loud
With the sawmill shrill of the locust, to the whole honey of
  the arid
  Sun. They are slow, proud,

And move with a stilted stride
To the land of sheer horizon, hunting Traherne's
Sensible emptiness, there where the brain's lantern-slide
  Revels in vast returns.

O connoisseurs of thirst,
Beasts of my soul who long to learn to drink
Of pure mirage, those prosperous islands are accurst
  That shimmer on the brink

Of absence; auras, lustres,
And all shinings need to be shaped and borne.
Think of those painted saints, capped by the early masters
  With bright, jauntily-worn

Aureate plates, or even
Merry-go-round rings. Turn, O turn
From the fine sleights of the sand, from the long empty oven
  Where flames in flamings burn

Back to the trees arrayed
In bursts of glare, to the halo-dialling run
Of the country creeks, and the hills' bracken tiaras made
  Gold in the sunken sun,

Wisely watch for the sight
Of the supernova burgeoning over the barn,
Lampshine blurred in the steam of beasts, the spirit's right
  Oasis, light incarnate.

Museum Piece

THE good grey guardians of art
Patrol the halls on spongy shoes,
Impartially protective, though
Perhaps suspicious of Toulouse.

Here dozes one against the wall,
Disposed upon a funeral chair.
A Degas dancer pirouettes
Upon the parting of his hair.

See how she spins! The grace is there,
But strain as well is plain to see.
Degas loved the two together:
Beauty joined to energy.

Edgar Degas purchased once
A fine El Greco, which he kept
Against the wall beside his bed
To hang his pants on while he slept.

After the Last Bulletins

AFTER the last bulletins the windows darken
And the whole city founders readily and deep,
Sliding on all its pillows
To the thronged Atlantis of personal sleep,

And the wind rises. The wind rises and bowls
The day's litter of news in the alleys. Trash
Tears itself on the railings,
Soars and falls with a soft crash,

Tumbles and soars again. Unruly flights
Scamper the park, and taking a statue for dead
Strike at the positive eyes,
Batter and flap the stolid head

And scratch the noble name. In empty lots
Our journals spiral in a fierce noyade
Of all we thought to think,
Or caught in corners cramp and wad

And twist our words. And some from gutters flail
Their tatters at the tired patrolman's feet,
Like all that fisted snow
That cried beside his long retreat

Damn you! damn you! to the emperor's horse's heels.
Oh none too soon through the air white and dry
Will the clear announcer's voice
Beat like a dove, and you and I

From the heart's anarch and responsible town
Return by subway-mouth to life again,
Bearing the morning papers,
And cross the park where saintlike men

White and absorbed, with stick and bag remove
The litter of the night, and footsteps rouse
With confident morning sound
The songbirds in the public boughs.

She

WHAT was her beauty in our first estate
When Adam's will was whole, and the least thing
Appeared the gift and creature of his king,
How should we guess? Resemblance had to wait

For separation, and in such a place
She so partook of water, light, and trees
As not to look like any one of these.
He woke and gazed into her naked face.

But then she changed, and coming down amid
The flocks of Abel and the fields of Cain,
Clothed in their wish, her Eden graces hid,
A shape of plenty with a mop of grain,

She broke upon the world, in time took on
The look of every labour and its fruits.
Columnar in a robe of pleated lawn
She cupped her patient hand for attributes,

Was radiant captive of the farthest tower
And shed her honour on the fields of war,
Walked in her garden at the evening hour,
Her shadow like a dark ogival door,

Breasted the seas for all the westward ships
And, come to virgin empires, changed again –
A moonlike being truest in eclipse
And subject goddess of the dreams of men.

Tree, temple, valley, prow, gazelle, machine,
More named and nameless than the morning star,
Lovely in every shape, in all unseen,
We dare not wish to find you as you are,

Whose apparition, biding time until
Desire decay and bring the latter age,
Shall flourish in the ruins of our will
And deck the broken stones like saxifrage.

The Undead

Even as children they were late sleepers,
Preferring their dreams, even when quick with monsters,
    To the world with all its breakable toys,
        Its compacts with the dying;

From the stretched arms of withered trees
They turned, fearing contagion of the mortal,
    And even under the plums of summer
        Drifted like winter moons.

Secret, unfriendly, pale, possessed
Of the one wish, the thirst for mere survival,
    They came, as all extremists do
        In time, to a sort of grandeur:

Now, to their Balkan battlements
Above the vulgar town of their first lives,
    They rise at the moon's rising. Strange
        That their utter self-concern

Should, in the end, have left them selfless:
Mirrors fail to perceive them as they float
    Through the great hall and up the staircase;
        Nor are the cobwebs broken.

Into the pallid night emerging,
Wrapped in their flapping capes, routinely maddened
    By a wolf's cry, they stand for a moment
        Stoking the mind's eye

With lewd thoughts of the pressed flowers
And bric-à-brac of rooms with something to lose,–
Of love-dismembered dolls, and children
Buried in quilted sleep.

Then they are off in a negative frenzy,
Their black shapes cropped into sudden bats
That swarm, burst, and are gone. Thinking
Of a thrush cold in the leaves

Who has sung his few summers truly,
Or an old scholar resting his eyes at last,
We cannot be much impressed with vampires,
Colourful though they are;

Nevertheless, their pain is real,
And requires our pity. Think how sad it must be
To thirst always for a scorned elixir,
The salt quotidian blood

Which, if mistrusted, has no savour;
To prey on life forever and not possess it,
As rock-hollows, tide after tide,
Glassily strand the sea.

In the Smoking Car

THE eyelids meet. He'll catch a little nap.
The grizzled, crew-cut head drops to his chest.
It shakes above the briefcase on his lap.
Close voices breathe, 'Poor sweet, he did his best.'

'Poor sweet, poor sweet,' the bird-hushed glades repeat,
Through which in quiet pomp his litter goes,
Carried by native girls with naked feet.
A sighing stream concurs in his repose.

Could he but think, he might recall to mind
The righteous mutiny or sudden gale
That beached him here; the dear ones left behind . . .
So near the ending, he forgets the tale.

Were he to lift his eyelids now, he might
Behold his maiden porters, brown and bare.
But even here he has no appetite.
It is enough to know that they are there.

Enough that now a honeyed music swells,
The gentle, mossed declivities begin,
And the whole air is full of flower-smells.
Failure, the longed-for valley, takes him in.

Shame

It is a cramped little state with no foreign policy,
Save to be thought inoffensive. The grammar of the language
Has never been fathomed, owing to the national habit
Of allowing each sentence to trail off in confusion.
Those who have visited Scusi, the capital city,
Report that the railway-route from Schuldig passes
Through country best described as unrelieved.
Sheep are the national product. The faint inscription
Over the city gates may perhaps be rendered,
'I'm afraid you won't find much of interest here.'
Census-reports which give the population
As zero are, of course, not to be trusted,
Save as reflecting the natives' flustered insistence
That they do not count, as well as their modest horror
Of letting one's sex be known in so many words.
The uniform grey of the nondescript buildings, the absence
Of churches or comfort-stations, have given observers
An odd impression of ostentatious meanness,

And it must be said of the citizens (muttering by
In their ratty sheepskins, shying at cracks in the sidewalk)
That they lack the peace of mind of the truly humble.
The tenor of life is careful, even in the stiff
Unsmiling carelessness of the border-guards
And *douaniers*, who admit, whenever they can,
Not merely the usual carloads of deodorant
But gypsies, g-strings, hasheesh, and contraband pigments.
Their complete negligence is reserved, however,
For the hoped-for invasion, at which time the happy people
(Sniggering, ruddily naked, and shamelessly drunk)
Will stun the foe by their overwhelming submission,
Corrupt the generals, infiltrate the staff,
Usurp the throne, proclaim themselves to be sun-gods,
And bring about the collapse of the whole empire.

Alceste in the Wilderness

Non, je ne puis souffrir cette lâche méthode
Qu'affectent la plupart de vos gens à la mode . . .
MOLIÈRE, *Le Misanthrope*

EVENING is clogged with gnats as the light fails,
And branches bloom with gold and copper screams
Of birds with figured and sought-after tails
To plume a lady's gear; the motet wails
Through Africa upon dissimilar themes.

A little snuffbox whereon Daphnis sings
In pale enamels, touching love's defeat,
Calls up the colour of her underthings
And plays upon the taut memorial strings,
Trailing her laces down into this heat.

One day he found, topped with a smutty grin,
The small corpse of a monkey, partly eaten.
Force of the sun had split the bluish skin,
Which, by their questioning and entering in,
A swarm of bees had been concerned to sweeten.

He could distill no essence out of this.
That yellow majesty and molten light
Should bless this carcass with a sticky kiss
Argued a brute and filthy emphasis.
The half-moons of the fingernails were white,

And where the nostrils opened on the skies,
Issuing to the sinus, where the ant
Crawled swiftly down to undermine the eyes
Of cloudy aspic, nothing could disguise
How terribly the thing looked like Philinte.

90

Will-o'-the-wisp, on the scum-laden water,
Burns in the night, a gaseous deceiver,
In the pale shade of France's foremost daughter.
Heat gives his thinking cavity no quarter,
For he is burning with the monkey's fever.

Before the bees have diagrammed their comb
Within the skull, before summer has cracked
The back of Daphnis, naked, polychrome,
Versailles shall see the tempered exile home,
Peruked and stately for the final act.

Samuel Sewall

SAMUEL SEWALL, in a world of wigs,
Flouted opinion in his personal hair;
For foppery he gave not any figs,
But in his right and honour took the air.

Thus in his naked style, though well attired,
He went forth in the city, or paid court
To Madam Winthrop, whom he much admired,
Most godly, but yet liberal with the port.

And all the town admired for two full years
His excellent address, his gifts of fruit,
Her gracious ways and delicate white ears,
And held the course of nature absolute.

But yet she bade him suffer a peruke,
'That One be not distinguished from the All';
Delivered of herself this stern rebuke
Framed in the resonant language of St Paul.

'Madam,' he answered her, 'I have a Friend
Furnishes me with hair out of His strength,
And He requires only I attend
Unto His charity and to its length.'

And all the town was witness to his trust:
On Monday he walked out with the Widow Gibbs,
A pious lady of charm and notable bust,
Whose heart beat tolerably beneath her ribs.

On Saturday he wrote proposing marriage,
And closed, imploring that she be not cruel,
'Your favourable answer will oblige,
Madam, your humble servant, Samuel Sewall.'

The Vow

IN the third month, a sudden flow of blood.
The mirth of tabrets ceaseth, and the joy
Also of the harp. The frail image of God
Lay spilled and formless. Neither girl nor boy,
But yet blood of my blood, nearly my child.
   All that long day
Her pale face turned to the window's mild
   Featureless grey.

And for some nights she whimpered as she dreamed
The dead thing spoke, saying: 'Do not recall
Pleasure at my conception. I am redeemed
From pain and sorrow. Mourn rather for all
Who breathlessly issue from the bone gates,
   The gates of horn,
For truly it is best of all the fates
   Not to be born.

'Mother, a child lay gasping for bare breath
On Christmas Eve when Santa Claus had set
Death in the stocking, and the lights of death
Flamed in the tree. O, if you can, forget
You were the child, turn to my father's lips
   Against the time
When his cold hand puts forth its fingertips
   Of jointed lime.'

Doctors of Science, what is man that he
Should hope to come to a good end? *The best
Is not to have been born.* And could it be
That Jewish diligence and Irish jest
The consent of flesh and a midwinter storm
   Had reconciled,
Was yet too bold a mixture to inform
   A simple child?

Even as gold is tried, Gentile and Jew.
If that ghost was a girl's, I swear to it:
Your mother shall be far more blessed than you.
And if a boy's, I swear: The flames are lit
That shall refine us; they shall not destroy
   A living hair.
Your younger brothers shall confirm in joy
   This that I swear.

The End of the Weekend

A DYING firelight slides along the quirt
Of the cast-iron cowboy where he leans
Against my father's books. The lariat
Whirls into darkness. My girl, in skin-tight jeans,
Fingers a page of Captain Marryat,
Inviting insolent shadows to her shirt.

We rise together to the second floor.
Outside, across the lake, an endless wind
Whips at the headstones of the dead and wails
In the trees for all who have and have not sinned.
She rubs against me and I feel her nails.
Although we are alone, I lock the door.

The eventual shapes of all our formless prayers,
This dark, this cabin of loose imaginings,
Wind, lake, lip, everything awaits
The slow unloosening of her underthings.
And then the noise. Something is dropped. It grates
Against the attic beams.
                              I climb the stairs
Armed with a belt.
                         A long magnesium strip
Of moonlight from the dormer cuts a path
Among the shattered skeletons of mice.
A great black presence beats its wings in wrath.
Above the boneyard burn its golden eyes.
Some small grey fur is pulsing in its grip.

'More Light! More Light!'

Composed in the Tower before his execution
These moving verses, and being brought at that time
Painfully to the stake, submitted, declaring thus:
'I implore my God to witness that I have made no crime.'

Nor was he forsaken of courage, but the death was horrible,
The sack of gunpowder failing to ignite.
His legs were blistered sticks on which the black sap
Bubbled and burst as he howled for the Kindly Light.

And that was but one, and by no means one of the worst;
Permitted at least his pitiful dignity;
And such as were by made prayers in the name of Christ,
That shall judge all men, for his soul's tranquillity.

We move now to outside a German wood.
Three men are there commanded to dig a hole
In which the two Jews are ordered to lie down
And be buried alive by the third, who is a Pole.

Not light from the shrine at Weimar beyond the hill
Nor light from heaven appeared. But he did refuse.
A Lüger settled back deeply in its glove.
He was ordered to change places with the Jews.

Much casual death had drained away their souls.
The thick dirt mounted toward the quivering chin.
When only the head was exposed the order came
To dig him out again and to get back in.

No light, no light in the blue Polish eye.
When he finished a riding boot packed down the earth.
The Lüger hovered lightly in its glove.
He was shot in the belly and in three hours bled to death.

No prayers or incense rose up in those hours
Which grew to be years, and every day came mute
Thousands sifting down through the crisp air
And settled upon his eyes in a black soot.

The Performance

THE last time I saw Donald Armstrong
He was staggering oddly off into the sun,
Going down, of the Philippine Islands.
I let my shovel fall, and put that hand
Above my eyes, and moved some way to one side
That his body might pass through the sun,

And I saw how well he was not
Standing there on his hands,
On his spindle-shanked forearms balanced,
Unbalanced, with his big feet looming and waving
In the great, untrustworthy air
He flew in each night, when it darkened.

Dust fanned in scraped puffs from the earth
Between his arms, and blood turned his face inside out,
To demonstrate its suppleness
Of veins, as he perfected his role.
Next day, he toppled his head off
On an island beach to the south,

And the enemy's two-handed sword
Did not fall from anyone's hands
At that miraculous sight,
As the head rolled over upon
Its wide-eyed face, and fell
Into the inadequate grave

He had dug for himself, under pressure.
Yet I put my flat hand to my eyebrows
Months later, to see him again

In the sun, when I learned how he died,
And imagined him, there,
Come, judged, before his small captors,

Doing all his lean tricks to amaze them—
The back somersault, the kip-up—
And at last, the stand on his hands,
Perfect, with his feet together,
His head down, evenly breathing,
As the sun poured up from the sea

And the headsman broke down
In a blaze of tears, in that light
Of the thin, long human frame
Upside down in its own strange joy,
And, if some other one had not told him,,
Would have cut off the feet

Instead of the head,
And if Armstrong had not presently risen
In kingly, round-shouldered attendance,
And then knelt down in himself
Beside his hacked, glittering grave, having done
All things in this iife that he could.

Hunting Civil War Relics at
Nimblewill Creek

As he moves the mine-detector
A few inches over the ground,
Making it vitally float
Among the ferns and weeds,
I come into this war
Slowly, with my one brother,
Watching his face grow deep
Between the earphones,

For I can tell
If we enter the buried battle
Of Nimblewill
Only by his expression.

Softly he wanders, parting
The grass with a dreaming hand.
No dead cry yet takes root
In his clapped ears
Or can be seen in his smile.
But underfoot I feel
The dead regroup,
The burst metals all in place,
The battle lines be drawn
Anew to include us
In Nimblewill,
And I carry the shovel and pick

More as if they were
Bright weapons that I bore.
A bird's cry breaks
In two, and into three parts.
We cross the creek; the cry
Shifts into another,
Nearer, bird, and is
Like the shout of a shadow —
Lived-with, appallingly close —
Or the soul, pronouncing
'Nimblewill':
Three tones; your being changes.

We climb the bank;
A faint light glows
On my brother's mouth.
I listen, as two birds fight
For a single voice, but he
Must be hearing the grave,

In pieces, all singing
To his clamped head,
For he smiles as if
He rose from the dead within
Green Nimblewill
And stood in his grandson's shape.

No shot from the buried war
Can kill me now,
For the dead have waited here
A hundred years to create
The look on a man's loved features,
While I stand, with
The same voice calling insanely
Like that of a sniper
Who throws down his rifle and yells
In the pure joy of missing me
At Nimblewill
And my brother beside me holds

A long-buried light on his lips.
I fall to my knees
To dig wherever he points,
To bring up mess-tin or bullet,
To go underground
Still singing, myself,
Like a hidden bird,
Or a man who renounces war,
Or one who shall lift up the past,
Not breathing 'Father,'
At Nimblewill,
But saying, 'Fathers! Fathers!'

Overland to the Islands

LET'S go – much as that dog goes,
intently haphazard. The
Mexican light on a day that
'smells like autumn in Connecticut'
makes iris ripples on his
black gleaming fur – and that too
is as one would desire – a radiance
consorting with the dance.
                              Under his feet
rocks and mud, his imagination, sniffing,
engaged in its perceptions – dancing
edgeways, there's nothing
the dog disdains on his way,
nevertheless he
keeps moving, changing
pace and approach but
not direction – 'every step an arrival'.

Sunday Afternoon

AFTER the First Communion
and the banquet of mangoes and
bridal cake, the young daughters
of the coffee merchant lay down
for a long siesta, and their white dresses
lay beside them in quietness
and the white veils floated
In their dreams as the flies buzzed.

But as the afternoon
burned to a close they rose
and ran about the neighbourhood
among the halfbuilt villas
alive, alive, kicking a basketball, wearing
other new dresses, of bloodred velvet.

The Springtime

THE red eyes of rabbits
aren't sad. No one passes
the sad golden village in a barge
any more. The sunset
will leave it alone. If the
curtains hang askew
it is no one's fault.
Around and around and around
everywhere the same sound
of wheels going, and things
growing older, growing
silent. If the dogs
bark to each other
all night, and their eyes
flash red, that's
nobody's business. They have
a great space of dark to
bark across. The rabbits
will bare their teeth at
the spring moon.

The Grace-note

IN Sabbath quiet, a street
of closed warehouses and wholesale silence,
Adam Misery, while the cop frisks him

lifts with both hands his lip and
drooping moustache to reveal
horse-teeth for inspection.

                              Nothing
is new to him and he is not afraid.
This is a world. As the artist

extends his world with
one gratuitous flourish – a stroke of white or
a run on the clarinet above the

base tones of the orchestra – so he
ornaments his with
fresh contempt.

The World Outside

I

ON the kitchen wall a flash
of shadow:
            swift pilgrimage
of pigeons, a spiral
celebration of air, of sky-deserts.
And on tenement windows
a blaze
         of lustred watermelon:
stain of the sun
westering somewhere back of Hoboken.

II

The goatherd upstairs! Music
from his sweet flute
roves from summer to summer
in the dusty air of airshafts
and among the flakes
of soot that float
in a daze from chimney
to chimney – notes
remote, cool, speaking of slender
shadows under olive-leaves. A silence.

III

Groans, sighs, in profusion,
with coughing, muttering, orchestrate
solitary grief; the crash of glass, a low voice
repeating over and over, 'No.
    No. I want my key. No you did not.
    No.' – a commonplace.
And in counterpoint, from other windows,
the effort to be merry – ay, maracas!
– sibilant, intricate – the voices wailing pleasure,
    arriving perhaps at joy, late, after sets
have been switched off, and silences
are dark windows?

Six Variations

I

WE have been shown
how Basket drank –
and old man Volpe the cobbler
made up what words he didn't know
so that his own son, even,
laughed at him: but with respect.

II

Two flutes! How close
to each other they move
in mazing figures,
never touching, never
breaking the measure,
as gnats dance in
summer haze all afternoon, over
shallow water sprinkled
with mottled blades of willow –
two flutes!

III

Shlup, shlup, the dog
as it laps up
water
makes intelligent
music, resting
now and then to
take breath in irregular
measure.

IV

When I can't
strike one spark from you,
when you don't
look me in the eye,
when your answers
come
          slowly, dragging
their feet, and furrows
change your face,
when the sky is a cellar
with dirty windows,
when furniture
obstructs the body, and bodies

are heavy furniture coated
with dust – time
for a lagging leaden pace,
a short sullen line,
measure
of heavy heart and
cold eye.

V

The quick of the sun that gilds
broken pebbles in sidewalk cement
and the iridescent
spit, that defiles and adorns!
Gold light in blind love does not distinguish
one surface from another, the savour
is the same to its tongue, the fluted
cylinder of a new ashcan a dazzling silver,
the smooth flesh of screaming children a
    quietness, it is all
a jubilance, the light catches up
the disordered street in its apron,
broken fruitrinds shine in the gutter.

VI

Lap up the vowels
of sorrow,
         transparent, cold
water-darkness welling
up from the white sand.
Hone the blade
of a scythe to cut swathes
of light sound in the mind.
Through the hollow globe, a ring
of frayed rusty scrapiron,
is it the sea that shines?
Is it a road at the world's edge?

A Map of the Western Part of the County of Essex in England

SOMETHING forgotten twenty years: though my fathers
and mothers came from Cordova and Vitepsk and Caer-
narvon,
and though I am a citizen of the United States and less a
stranger here than anywhere else, perhaps,
I am Essex-born:
Cranbrook Wash called me into its dark tunnel,
the little streams of Valentines heard my resolves,
Roding held my head above water when I thought it was
drowning me; in Hainault only a haze of thin trees
stood between the red doubledecker buses and the boar-
hunt,
the spirit of merciful Phillippa glimmered there.
Pergo Park knew me, and Clavering, and Havering-atte-
Bower,
Stanford Rivers lost me in osier-beds, Stapleford Abbots
sent me safe home on the dark road after Simeon-quiet
evensong,
Wanstead drew me over and over into its basic poetry,
in its serpentine lake I saw bass-viols among the golden dead
leaves,
through its trees the ghost of a great house. In
Ilford High Road I saw the multitudes passing pale under
the
light of flaring sundown, seven kings
in sombre starry robes gathered at Seven Kings
the place of law
where my birth and marriage are recorded
and the death of my father. Woodford Wells
where an old house was named The Naked Beauty (a white
statue forlorn in its garden)
saw the meeting and parting of two sisters
(forgotten? and further away

the hill before Thaxted? where peace befell us? not once
but many times?)
All the Ivans dreaming of their villages
all the Marias dreaming of their walled cities,
picking up fragments of New World slowly
not knowing how to put them together nor how to join
image with image, now I know how it was with you, an old
   map
made long before I was born shows ancient
rights of way where I walked when I was ten burning with
   desire
for the world's great splendours, a child who traced voyages
indelibly all over the atlas, who now in a far country
remembers the first river, the first
field, bricks, and lumber dumped in it ready for building,
that new smell, and remembers
the walls of the garden, the first light.

The Picnic

It is the picnic with Ruth in the spring.
Ruth was third on my list of seven girls
But the first two were gone (Betty) or else
Had someone (Ellen has accepted Doug).
Indian Gully the last day of school;
Girls make the lunches for the boys too.
I wrote a note to Ruth in algebra class
Day before the test. She smiled, and nodded.
We left the cars and walked through the young corn
The shoots green as paint and the leaves like tongues
Trembling. Beyond the fence where we stood
Some wild strawberry flowered by an elm tree
And Jack-in-the-pulpit was olive ripe.
A blackbird fled as I crossed, and showed
A spot of gold or red under its quick wing.
I held the wire for Ruth and watched the whip
Of her long, striped skirt as she followed.
Three freckles blossomed on her thin, white back
Underneath the loop where the blouse buttoned.
We went for our lunch away from the rest,
Stretched in the new grass, our heads close
Over unknown things wrapped up in wax papers.
Ruth tried for the same, I forget what it was,
And our hands were together. She laughed,
And a breeze caught the edge of her little
Collar and the edge of her brown, loose hair
That touched my cheek. I turned my face in-
to the gentle fall. I saw how sweet it smelled.
She didn't move her head or take her hand.
I felt a soft caving in my stomach

As at the top of the highest slide
When I had been a child, but was not afraid,
And did not know why my eyes moved with wet
As I brushed her cheek with my lips and brushed
Her lips with my own lips. She said to me
Jack, Jack, different than I had ever heard,
Because she wasn't calling me, I think,
Or telling me. She used my name to
Talk in another way I wanted to know.
She laughed again and then she took her hand;
I gave her what we both had touched – can't
Remember what it was, and we ate the lunch.
Afterward we walked in the small, cool creek
Our shoes off, her skirt hitched, and she smiling,
My pants rolled, and then we climbed up the high
Side of Indian Gully and looked
Where we had been, our hands together again.
It was then some bright thing came in my eyes,
Starting at the back of them and flowing
Suddenly through my head and down my arms
And stomach and my bare legs that seemed not
To stop in feet, not to feel the red earth
Of the Gully, as though we hung in a
Touch of birds. There was a word in my throat
With the feeling and I knew the first time
What it meant and I said, it's beautiful.
Yes, she said, and I felt the sound and word
In my hand join the sound and word in hers
As in one name said, or in one cupped hand.
We put back on our shoes and socks and we
Sat in the grass awhile, crosslegged, under
A blowing tree, not saying anything.
And Ruth played with shells she found in the creek,
As I watched. Her small wrist which was so sweet
To me turned by her breast and the shells dropped
Green, white, blue, easily into her lap,

Passing light through themselves. She gave the pale
Shells to me, and got up and touched her hips
With her light hands, and we walked down slowly
To play the school games with the others.

A Trip to Four or Five Towns
(To James Wright)

I

THE gold-coloured skin of my Lebanese friends.
Their deep, lightless eyes.
The serene, inner, careful
balance they share. The conjugal
smile of either for either.

II

This bellychilling, shoe soaking, factory-
dug-up-hill smothering Pittsburgh weather!
I wait for a cab in the smart mahogany
lobby of the seminary.
The marble *Pietà* is flanked around
with fake fern. She cherishes her dead son
stretched along her womb he triple crossed.
A small, slippered priest
pads up. Whom do you seek, my son?
Father, I've come in out of the rain.
I seek refuge from the elemental tears,
for my heavy, earthen body runs to grief
and I am apt to drown
in this small and underhanded rain
that drops its dross so delicately
on the hairs of the flowers, my father,
and follows down the veins of leaves
weeping quiet in the wood.

My yellow cab never came,
but I did not confess
beneath the painted Jesus Christ. I left
and never saved myself at all
That night in that late, winter rain.

III

In Washington, was it spring?
I took the plane.
I heard, on either side,
the soft executives, manicured and
fat, fucking this and fucking that.
My heavy second breakfast
lay across my lap.
At port, in the great concourse,
I could not walk to city bus
or cab? or limousine?
I sweat with shock, with havoc
Of the hundred kinds of time,
trembling like a man away from home.

At the National Stripshow
where the girls wriggle right
and slow, I find I want to see in
under the sequin step in.
And in my later dream of the negro girl's room
strong with ancient sweat and with her thick
aroma, I seem to play a melodrama
as her great, red dog barks twice
and I stab it with my pocket knife.

IV

In Richmond the azalea banks
burst in rose and purple gullies by the car,
muted in the soft, wet

April twilight. The old estates
were pruned and rolled fresh
with spring, with splendour, touch-
ing the graceful stride of the boy who brings the paper.

v

My friend has a red-headed mother
capable of love in any kind
of weather. I am not sure
what she passes to her daughters
but from her brown eye and from her breast
she passes wit and spunk to her big sons.
And she is small and pleased when they put
their arms around her, having caught her.
They cut the grass naked to the waist.
They cure the handsome skins of chipmunks and of snakes.
And when they wake in their attic room
they climb down the ladder, half
asleep, feeling the rungs' pressure
on their bare feet, shirt tails out,
brown eyes shut. They eat
what she cooks. One shot a gorgeous coloured hawk
and posed with it, proud, arms and full wings
spread. And one, at the beach,
balanced on his hands, posed
stripped, in the void of sand,
limbs a rudder in the wind,
amid the lonely, blasted wood.
And two sons run swift roans in the high, summer grass.
Now I would guess
her daughters had at least this same
grace and beauty as their mother,
though I have only seen their picture.
I know she is happy with her three
strong sons about her, for they are not clumsy
(one, calmed, so calmly,

bends a good ear to his guitar)
and they are not dull:
one built a small electric shaft topped with a glowing ball.

VI

In New York I got drunk, to tell the truth,
and almost got locked up when a beat
friend with me took a leak in a telephone booth.
(E. E. Cummings on the Paris lawn.
'Reprieve pisseur Américain!')
At two o'clock he got knocked out
horning in with the girl in the room over him.
Her boy friend was still sober,
and too thin. I saw the blood of a poet
flow on the sidewalk. Oh, if I mock,
it is without heart. I thought
of the torn limbs of Orpheus
scattered in the grass on the hills of Thrace.
Do poets have to have such trouble with the female race?
I do not know. But if they bleed
I lose heart also.
When he reads, ah, when he reads, small but deep-voiced,
he reads well: now weeps, now is cynical,
his large, horned eyes very black and tearful.

And when we visited a poet father
we rode to Jersey on a motor scooter.
My tie and tweeds looped in the winds
I choked in the wake
of the Holland Pipe, and cops,
under glass like carps, eyed us.
That old father was so mellow and generous –
easy to pain,
white, open and at peace, and of good taste,
like his Rutherford house.
And he read, very loud and regal,
sixteen new poems based on paintings by Breughel!

VII

The last night out,
before I climbed on the formal
Capital Viscount and was shot home
high, pure, and clear,
seemed like the right time
to disappear.

Early in the Morning

EARLY in the morning
The dark Queen said,
'The trumpets are warning
There's trouble ahead.'
Spent with carousing,
With wine-soaked wits,
Antony drowsing
Whispered, 'It's
Too cold a morning
To get out of bed.'

The army's retreating,
The fleet has fled,
Caesar is beating
His drums through the dead.
'Antony, horses!
We'll get away,
Gather our forces
For another day . . .'
'It's a cold morning,'
Antony said.

Caesar Augustus
Cleared his phlegm.
'Corpses disgust us.
Cover them.'
Caesar Augustus
In his time lay
Dying, and just as
Cold as they,
On the cold morning
Of a cold day.

115

The Ash and the Oak

WHEN men discovered freedom first
The fighting was on foot,
They were encouraged by their thirst
And promises of loot,
And when it feathered and bows boomed
Their virtue was a root.

O the ash and the oak and the willow tree
And green grows the grass on the infantry!

At Malplaquet and Waterloo
They were polite and proud,
They primed their guns with billets-doux
And, as they fired, bowed.
At Appomattox too, it seems
Some things were understood.

O the ash and the oak and the willow tree
And green grows the grass on the infantry!

But at Verdun and at Bastogne
There was a great recoil,
The blood was bitter to the bone
The trigger to the soul,
And death was nothing if not dull,
A hero was a fool.

O the ash and the oak and the willow tree
And that's an end of the infantry!

To the Western World

A SIREN sang, and Europe turned away
From the high castle and the shepherd's crook.
Three caravels went sailing to Cathay
On the strange ocean, and the captains shook
Their banners out across the Mexique Bay.

And in our early days we did the same.
Remembering our fathers in their wreck
We crossed the sea from Palos where they came
And saw, enormous to the little deck,
A shore in silence waiting for a name.

The treasures of Cathay were never found.
In this America, this wilderness
Where the axe echoes with a lonely sound,
The generations labour to possess
And grave by grave we civilize the ground.

The Riders Held Back

ONE morning, as we travelled in the fields
    Of air and dew
With trumpets, and above the painted shields
    The banners flew,

We came upon three ladies, wreathed in roses,
    Where, hand in hand,
They danced – three slender, gentle, naked ladies,
    All in a woodland.

They'd been to the best schools in Italy;
    Their legs were Greek,
Their collarbones, as fine as jewellery,
    Their eyes, antique.

'Why do lambs skip and shepherds shout "Ut hoy!"?
　　　Why do you dance?'
Said one, 'It is an intellectual joy,
　　　The Renaissance.

'As do the stars in heaven, ruled by Three,
　　　We twine and move.
It is the music of Astronomy,
　　　Not men, we love.

'And as we dance, the beasts and flowers do;
　　　The fields of wheat
Sway like our arms; the curving hills continue
　　　The curves of our feet.

'Here Raphael comes to paint; the thrushes flute
　　　To Petrarch's pen.
But Michael is not here, who carved the brute
　　　Unfinished men.'

They danced again, and on the mountain heights
　　　There seemed to rise
Towers and ramparts glittering with lights,
　　　Like Paradise.

How the bright morning passed, I cannot say.
　　　We woke and found
The dancers gone; and heard, far, far away,
　　　The trumpet sound.

We galloped to it. In the forest then
　　　Banners and shields
Were strewn like leaves; and there were many slain
　　　In the dark fields.

Walt Whitman at Bear Mountain

*'... life which does not give the preference to any other life, of any
previous period, which therefore prefers its own existence ...'*

ORTEGA Y GASSET

NEITHER on horseback nor seated,
But like himself, squarely on two feet,
The poet of death and lilacs
Loafs by the footpath. Even the bronze looks alive
Where it is folded like cloth. And he seems friendly.

'Where is the Mississippi panorama
And the girl who played the piano?
Where are you, Walt?
The Open Road goes to the used-car lot.

'Where is the nation you promised?
These houses built of wood sustain
Colossal snows,
And the light above the street is sick to death.

'As for the people – see how they neglect you!
Only a poet pauses to read the inscription.'

'I am here,' he answered.
'It seems you have found me out.
Yet, did I not warn you that it was Myself
I advertised? Were my words not sufficiently plain?

'I gave no prescriptions,
And those who have taken my moods for prophecies
Mistake the matter.'
Then, vastly amused – 'Why do you reproach me?
I freely confess I am wholly disreputable.
Yet I am happy, because you have found me out.'

A crocodile in wrinkled metal loafing ...

Then all the realtors,
Pickpockets, salesmen, and the actors performing

Official scenarios,
Turned a deaf ear, for they had contracted
American dreams.

But the man who keeps a store on a lonely road,
And the housewife who knows she's dumb,
And the earth, are relieved.

All that grave weight of America
Cancelled! Like Greece and Rome.
The future in ruins!
The castles, the prisons, the cathedrals
Unbuilding, and roses
Blossoming from the stones that are not there . . .

The clouds are lifting from the high Sierras,
The Bay mists clearing;
And the angel in the gate, the flowering plum,
Dances like Italy, imagining red.

There Is

I

Look! From my window there's a view
of city streets
where only lives as dry as tortoises
can crawl – the Gallapagos of desire.

There is the day of Negroes with red hair
and the day of insane women on the subway;
there is the day of the word Trieste
and the night of the blind man with the electric guitar.

But I have no profession. Like a spy
I read the papers – Situations Wanted.
Surely there is a secret
which, if I knew it, would change everything!

II

I have the poor man's nerve-tic, irony.
I see through the illusions of the age!
The bell tolls, and the hearse advances,
and the mourners follow, for my entertainment.

I tread the burning pavement,
the streets where drunkards stretch
like photographs of civil death
and trumpets strangle in electric shelves.

The mannequins stare at me scornfully.
I know they are pretending
all day to be in earnest.
And can it be that love is an illusion?

When darkness falls on the enormous street
the air is filled with Eros, whispering.
Eyes, mouths, contrive to meet
in silence, fearing they may be prevented.

III

O businessmen like ruins,
bankers who are Bastilles,
widows, sadder than the shores of lakes,
then you were happy, when you still could tremble!

But all night long my window
sheds tears of light.
I seek the word. The word is not forthcoming.
O syllables of light . . . O dark cathedral . . .

My Father in the Night Commanding No

My father in the night commanding No
Has work to do. Smoke issues from his lips;
  He reads in silence.
The frogs are croaking and the streetlamps glow.

And then my mother winds the gramophone;
The Bride of Lammermoor begins to shriek –
  Or reads a story
About a prince, a castle, and a dragon.

The moon is glittering above the hill.
I stand before the gateposts of the King –
  So runs the story –
Of Thule, at midnight when the mice are still.

And I have been in Thule! It has come true –
The journey and the danger of the world,
  All that there is
To bear and to enjoy, endure and do.

Landscapes, seascapes . . . where have I been led?
The names of cities – Paris, Venice, Rome –
  Held out their arms.
A feathered god, seductive, went ahead.

Here is my house. Under a red rose tree
A child is swinging; another gravely plays.
  They are not surprised
That I am here; they were expecting me.

And yet my father sits and reads in silence,
My mother sheds a tear, the moon is still,
  And the dark wind
Is murmuring that nothing ever happens.

Beyond his jurisdiction as I move
Do I not prove him wrong? And yet, it's true
    They will not change
There, on the stage of terror and of love.

The actors in that playhouse always sit
In fixed positions – father, mother, child
    With painted eyes.
How sad it is to be a little puppet!

Their heads are wooden. And you once pretended
To understand them! Shake them as you will,
    They cannot speak.
Do what you will, the comedy is ended.

Father, why did you work? Why did you weep,
Mother? Was the story so important?
    '*Listen!*' the wind
Said to the children, and they fell asleep.

The Mountain Cemetery

WITH their harsh leaves old rhododendrons fill
The crevices in grave plots' broken stones.
The bees renew the blossoms they destroy,
While in the burning air the pines rise still,
Commemorating long forgotten biers,
Whose roots replace the semblance of these bones.

The weight of cool, of imperceptible dust
That came from nothing and to nothing came
Is light within the earth and on the air.
The change that so renews itself is just.
The enormous, sundry platitude of death
Is for these bones, bees, trees, and leaves the same.

And splayed upon the ground and through the trees
The mountains' shadow fills and cools the air,
Smoothing the shape of headstones to the earth.
The rhododendrons suffer with the bees
Whose struggles loose ripe petals to the earth,
The heaviest burden it shall ever bear.

Our hard earned knowledge fits us for such sleep.
Although the spring must come, it passes too
To form the burden suffered for what comes.
Whatever we would give our souls to keep
Is only part of what we call the soul;
What we of time would threaten to undo

All time in its slow scrutiny has done.
For on the grass that starts about the feet
The body's shadow turns, to shape in time,
Soon grown preponderant with creeping shade,
The final shadow that is turn of earth;
And what seems won paid for as in defeat.

The Prince

... si quid mea carmina possunt, nulla dies umquam memori vos eximet aevo, dum domus Aeneae Capitoli immobile saxum accolet ...

I COME to tell you that my son is dead.
Americans have shot him as a spy.
Our heritage has wasted what it shaped,
And he the ruin's proof. I suffered once
My self-destruction like a pleasure, gave
Over to what I could not understand
The one whom all my purpose was to save.
Deceit was the desire to be deceived,
For, when I kissed illusion's face, tears gushed
Warm under anguished eye-lids, and were dried
By new desire that chilled me like a wind –
As if it were defeat being alive
And hurt should yet restore me and be joy,
Joy without cause! Longing without an end,
That could not love the thing which it desired.
Through all that time I craved magnificence
Of the doomed fox – black paws, white throat, and red
Coat dragged among crisp yellow leaves, along
A stream trout break all night with glistening rise,
Austere, old lonely grandeur's complete pride
The pack's mute victim, while the crimson eyes
Glitter with Epicurus's innocence.
Giddy with lack of hope, my mind foresaw
Itself, still barely human and by duress
Bound in heroic trance, take glittering
Impassive armour up and crowd the niche
Of time with iron necessity; and hard
With loss and disbelief approved its choice.

This is the time's presumption: ignorance
Denies what we have been and might become.
So will and thought are mirrors of themselves.

125

Uniquely the strange object I might know,
I chose to live, who else had found no reason
In vanity's contempt, by simple faith
In what had been before me, and restored
The name of duty to a shadow, spent
Of meaning and obscure with rage and doubt
Intense as cold. My son, who was the heir
To every hope and trust, grew out of caring
Into the form of loss as I had done,
And then betrayed me who betrayed him first.
You know despair's authority, the rite
And exaltation by which we are governed,
A state absurd with wrath that we are human,
Nothing, to which our nature would submit.
Such was the German state. Yet, like a fool,
I hated it, my image, and was glad
When he refused its service; now I know
That even his imprisonment was mine,
A gesture by the will to break the will.
Honouring it, I dreamed again the fierce
Abandonment to what one hates, the fox
Joyful in pain and helplessness. O sages,
Of whom we are the merest shades, you are
The undemanding whom indifference
Has least defiled, those few whose innocence
Is earned by long distraction with minute
And slow corruption proving all they know,
Till patience, young in what may come to pass,
Is reconciled to what its love permits,
And is not proud that knowledge must be so.

*

By what persuasion he saw fit to change
Allegiance, none need wonder. Let there be,
However, no mistake: those who deny
What they believe is true, desire shall mock
And crime's uncertain promise shall deceive.

Alas, that he was not a German soldier
In his apostasy, but would put on
The parody of what caprice put off,
Enemy in disguise, the uniform
And speech of what the sceptic heart requires —
Ruthless the irony that is its thought!
The soldier's death should find him unaware,
The breathless air close round him as sleep falls,
Sudden with ripeness, heavy with release.
Thereby the guileless tranquilly are strong:
The man is overwhelmed, the deed remains.
Flesh of my flesh, bewildered to despair
And fallen outside the limits of my name,
Forever lies apart and meaningless.
I who remain perceive the dear, familiar
Unblemished face of possibility
Drenched by a waste profound with accident,
His childhood face concealed behind my face.
Where is the guile enough to comfort me?

The Centaur Overheard

ONCE I lived with my brothers, images
Of what we know best and can best become.
What I might be I learned to tell in eyes
Which loved me. Voices formed my name,

Taught me its sound, released me from its dread.
Now they are all gone. When I move, the sound
From dark caves where my hooves disturb the dead
Orders no other purpose. Underground,

Streams urge their ceaseless motion into air.
I stand by springs and drink. Their brimming poise
Repeats the selfish hope of who comes there.
But I do not look, move, or make a noise.

Adam's Song to Heaven

'You will be as God, knowing good and evil'

O DEPTH sufficient to desire,
Ghostly abyss wherein perfection hides,
   Purest effect and cause, you are
The mirror and the image love provides.

   All else is waste, though you reveal
Lightly upon your luminous bent shore
   Colour, shape, odour, weight, and voice,
Bright mocking hints that were not there before,

   And all your progeny time holds
In timeless birth and death. But, when, for bliss,
   Loneliness would possess its like,
Mine is the visage yours leans down to kiss.

   Beautiful you are, fair deceit!
Knowledge is joy where your unseeing eyes
   Shine with the tears that I have wept
To be the sum of all your thoughts devise.

   Flawless you are, unlimited
By other than yourself, yet suffer pain
   Of the nostalgias I have felt
For love beyond the end your eyes contain;

   Then, solitary, drift, inert,
Through the abyss where you would have me go,
   And, lost to your desire, at last
Ravish the waste for what you cannot know.

   What are you then! Delirium
Receives the image I despair to keep,
   And knowledge in your sombre depth
Embraces your perfection and your sleep.

Le Rêve

I DREAMED last night I dreamed, and in that sleep
You called me from the stair, as if the dead
Command all fragile sleepers to awake
And free them from their darkened wandering.
I knew that you would come into the room.
I waited for the sudden tug and slant
Upon the edge of my vague spectral bed,
The mattress tilted down, the springs gone tense.
I woke, looked at my watch, and sucked my breath.
There in my stead, still waiting, and still true,
Lay him who dreamed me still and, maybe, you.

And When the Green Man Comes

THE man is clothed
in birchbark,
small birds cling to his limbs
and one builds
a nest in his ear.

The clamor of bedlam
infests his hair, a wind
blowing in his head
shakes down
a thought that turns
to moss and lichen
at his feet.

His eyes are blind
with April,
his breath distilled
of butterflies
and bees, and in his beard
the maggot sings.

He comes again
with litter of chips
and empty cans,
his shoes full of mud and dung;

an army of shedding dogs
attends him,
the valley shudders where
he stands,
            redolent of roses,
exalted in
the streaming rain.

The Tundra

THE tundra is a living
body, warm in the grassy
autumn sun; it gives off
the odor of crushed
blueberries and gunsmoke.

In the tangled lakes
of its eyes a mirror of ice
is forming, where
frozen gut-piles shine
with a dull, rosy light.

Coarse, laughing men
with their women;
one by one the tiny campfires
flaring under the wind.

Full of blood, with a sound
like clicking hoofs,
the heavy tundra slowly
rolls over and sinks
in the darkness.

Foreboding

SOMETHING immense and lonely
divides the earth at evening.

For nine years I have watched
from an inner doorway:
as in a confused vision,
manlike figures approach, cover
their faces, and pass on,
heavy with iron and distance.

There is no sound but the wind
crossing the road, filling
the ruts with a dust as fine as chalk.

Like the closing of an inner door,
the day begins its dark
journey, across nine bridges
wrecked one by one.

If the Owl Calls Again

At dusk
from the island in the river,
and it's not too cold,

I'll wait for the moon
to rise,
then take wing and glide
to meet him.

We will not speak,
but hooded against the frost
soar above
the alder flats, searching
with tawny eyes.

And then we'll sit
in the shadowy spruce and
pick the bones
of careless mice,

while the long moon drifts
towards Asia
and the river mutters
in its icy bed.

And when morning climbs
the limbs
we'll part without a sound,

fulfilled, floating
homeward as
the cold world awakens.

To Turn Back

THE grass people bow
their heads before the wind.

How would it be
to stand among them, bending
our heads like that . . . ?

Yes . . . and no . . . perhaps . . .
lifting our dusty faces
as if we were waiting for
the rain . . . ?

The grass people stand
all year, patient and obedient —

to be among them
is to have only simple
and friendly thoughts,

and not be afraid.

Beyond the Hunting Woods

I SPEAK of that great house
Beyond the hunting woods,
Turreted and towered
In nineteenth-century style,
Where fireflies by the hundreds
Leap in the long grass,
Odour of jessamine
And roses, canker-bit,
Recalling famous times
When dame and maiden sipped
Sassafras or wild
Elderberry wine,
While far in the hunting woods
Men after their red hounds
Pursued the mythic beast.

I ask it of a stranger,
In all that great house finding
Not any living thing,
Or of the wind and the weather,
What charm was in that wine
That they should vanish so,
Ladies in their stiff
Bone and clean of limb,
And over the hunting woods
What mist had maddened them
That gentlemen should lose
Not only the beast in view
But Belle and Ginger too,
Nor home from the hunting woods
Ever, ever come?

On the Death of Friends in Childhood

WE shall not ever meet them bearded in heaven,
Nor sunning themselves among the bald of hell;
If anywhere, in the deserted schoolyard at twilight,
Forming a ring, perhaps, or joining hands
In games whose very names we have forgotten.
Come, memory, let us seek them there in the shadows.

Here in Katmandu

WE have climbed the mountain
There's nothing more to do.
It is terrible to come down
To the valley
Where, amidst many flowers,
One thinks of snow,

As, formerly, amidst snow,
Climbing the mountain,
One thought of flowers,
Tremulous, ruddy with dew,
In the valley.
One caught their scent coming down.

It is difficult to adjust, once down,
To the absence of snow.
Clear days, from the valley,
One looks up at the mountain.
What else is there to do?
Prayerwheels, flowers!

Let the flowers
Fade, the prayerwheels run down.
What have these to do

With us who have stood atop the snow
Atop the mountain,
Flags seen from the valley?

It might be possible to live in the valley,
To bury oneself among flowers,
If one could forget the mountain,
How, setting out before dawn,
Blinded with snow,
One knew what to do.

Meanwhile it is not easy here in Katmandu,
Especially when to the valley
That wind which means snow
Elsewhere, but here means flowers,
Comes down,
As soon it must, from the mountain.

Another Song

MERRY the green, the green hill shall be merry.
Hungry, the owlet shall seek out the mouse,
And Jack his Joan, but they shall never marry.

And snows shall fly, the big flakes fat and furry.
Lonely, the traveller shall seek out the house,
And Jack his Joan, but they shall never marry.

Weary the soldiers go, and come back weary,
Up a green hill and down the withered hill,
And Jack from Joan, and they shall never marry.

Counting the Mad

THIS one was put in a jacket,
This one was sent home,
This one was given bread and meat
But would eat none,
And this one cried No No No No
All day long.

This one looked at the window
As though it were a wall,
This one saw things that were not there,
This one things that were,
And this one cried No No No No
All day long.

This one thought himself a bird,
This one a dog,
And this one thought himself a man,
An ordinary man,
And cried and cried No No No No
All day long.

On a Painting by Patient B of the Independence
State Hospital for the Insane

I

THESE seven houses have learned to face one another,
But not at the expected angles. Those silly brown lumps,
That are probably meant for hills and not other houses,
After ages of being themselves, though naturally slow,
Are learning to be exclusive without offending.
The arches and entrances (down to the right out of sight)
Have mastered the lesson of remaining closed.
And even the skies keep a certain understandable distance,
For these are the houses of the very rich.

II

One sees their children playing with leopards, tamed
At great cost, or perhaps it is only other children,
For none of these objects is anything more than a spot,
And perhaps there are not any children but only leopards
Playing with leopards, and perhaps there are only the spots.
And the little maids from the windows hanging like tongues,
Calling the children in, admiring the leopards,
Are the dashes a child might represent motion by means of,
Or dazzlement possibly, the brilliance of solid-gold houses.

III

The clouds resemble those empty balloons in cartoons
Which approximate silence. These clouds, if clouds they are
(And not the smoke from the seven aspiring chimneys),
The more one studies them the more it appears
They too have expressions. One might almost say
They have their habits, their wrong opinions, that their
Impassivity masks an essentially lovable foolishness,
And they will be given names by those who live under them
Not public like mountains' but private like companions'.

Where We Must Look for Help

THE dove returns; it found no resting place;
It was in flight all night above the shaken seas;
Beneath ark eaves
The dove shall magnify the tiger's bed;
Give the dove peace.
The split-tail swallows leave the sill at dawn;
At dusk, blue swallows shall return.
On the third day the crow shall fly;
The crow, the crow, the spider-coloured crow,
The crow shall find new mud to walk upon.

Sunday in Glastonbury

IT is out in the flimsy suburbs,
Where the light seems to shine through the walls.

My black shoes stand on the floor
Like two open graves.

The curtains do not know what to hope for,
But they are obedient.

How strange to think of India!
Wealth is nothing but lack of people.

Awakening

WE are approaching sleep: the chestnut blossoms in the
   mind
Mingle with thoughts of pain
And the long roots of barley, bitterness
As of the oak roots staining the waters dark
In Louisiana, the wet streets soaked with rain
And sodden blossoms, out of this
We have come, a tunnel softly hurtling into darkness.

The storm is coming. The small farmhouse in Minnesota
Is hardly strong enough for the storm.
Darkness, darkness in grass, darkness in trees.
Even the water in wells trembles.
Bodies give off darkness, and chrysanthemums
Are dark, and horses, who are bearing great loads of hay
To the deep barns where the dark air is moving from corners.

Lincoln's statue and the traffic. From the long past
Into the long present
A bird, forgotten in these pressures, warbling,
As the great wheel turns around, grinding
The living in water.
Washing, continual washing, in water now stained
With blossoms and rotting logs,
Cries, half-muffled, from beneath the earth, the living
   awakened at last like the dead.

Poem Against the British

I

THE wind through the box-elder trees
Is like rides at dusk on a white horse,
Wars for your country, and fighting the British.

II

I wonder if Washington listened to the trees.
All morning I have been sitting in grass,
Higher than my eyes, beneath trees,
And listening upward, to the wind in leaves.
Suddenly I realize there is one thing more:
There is also the wind through the high grass.

III

There are palaces, boats, silence among white buildings,
Iced drinks on marble tops among cool rooms;
It is also good to be poor, and listen to the wind.

Driving toward the Lac Qui Parle River

I

I AM driving; it is dusk; Minnesota.
The stubble field catches the last growth of sun.
The soybeans are breathing on all sides.
Old men are sitting before their houses on carseats
In the small towns. I am happy,
The moon rising above the turkey sheds.

II

The small world of the car
Plunges through the deep fields of the night,
On the road from Willmar to Milan.

This solitude covered with iron
Moves through the fields of night
Penetrated by the noise of crickets.

III

Nearly to Milan, suddenly a small bridge,
And water kneeling in the moonlight.
In small towns the houses are built right on the ground;
The lamplight falls on all fours in the grass.
When I reach the river, the full moon covers it;
A few people are talking low in a boat.

Hunting Pheasants in a Cornfield

I

WHAT is so strange about a tree alone in an open field?
It is a willow tree. I walk around and around it.
The body is strangely torn, and cannot leave it.
At last I sit down beneath it.

II

It is a willow tree alone in acres of dry corn.
Its leaves are scattered around its trunk, and around me,
Brown now, and speckled with delicate black.
Only the cornstalks now can make a noise.

III

The sun is cold, burning through the frosty distances of space.
The weeds are frozen to death long ago.
Why then do I love to watch
The sun moving on the chill skin of the branches?

IV

The mind has shed leaves alone for years.
It stands apart with small creatures near its roots.
I am happy in this ancient place,
A spot easily caught sight of above the corn,
If I were a young animal ready to turn home at dusk.

A Busy Man Speaks

Not to the mother of solitude will I give myself
Away, not to the mother of art, nor the mother
Of the ocean, nor the mother of the snake and the fire;
Not to the mother of love,
Nor the mother of conversation, nor the mother
Of the downcast face, nor the mother of the solitude of
    death;
Not to the mother of the night full of crickets,
Nor the mother of the open fields, nor the mother of Christ.

But I will give myself to the father of righteousness, the
    father
Of cheerfulness, who is also the father of rocks,
Who is also the father of perfect gestures;
From the Chase National Bank
An arm of flame has come, and I am drawn
To the desert, to the parched places, to the landscape of
    zeros;
And I shall give myself away to the father of righteousness,
The stones of cheerfulness, the steel of money, the father of
    rocks.

Poem in Three Parts

I

OH, on an early morning I think I shall live forever!
I am wrapped in my joyful flesh,
As the grass is wrapped in its clouds of green.

II

Rising from a bed, where I dreamt
Of long rides past castles and hot coals,
The sun lies happily on my knees;
I have suffered and survived the night,
Bathed in dark water, like any blade of grass.

III

The strong leaves of the box-elder tree,
Plunging in the wind, call us to disappear
Into the wilds of the universe,
Where we shall sit at the foot of a plant,
And live forever, like the dust.

The Possibility of New Poetry

SINGING of Niagara, and the Huron squaws,
The chaise-longue, the periwinkles in a rage like snow,
Dillinger like a dark wind.
Intelligence, cover the advertising men with clear water,
And the factories with merciless space,
So that the strong-haunched woman
By the blazing stove of the sun, the moon,
May come home to me, sitting on the naked wood
In another world, and all the Shell stations
Folded in a faint light.

After the Industrial Revolution,
All Things Happen at Once

Now we enter a strange world, where the Hessian Christmas
Still goes on, and Washington has not reached the other
  shore;
The Whiskey Boys
Are gathering again on the meadows of Pennsylvania
And the Republic is still sailing on the open sea

In 1956 I saw a black angel in Washington, dancing
On a barge, saying, 'Let us now divide kennel dogs
And hunting dogs'; Henry Cabot Lodge, in New York,
Talking of sugar cane in Cuba; Ford,
In Detroit, drinking mother's milk;
Henry Cabot Lodge, saying, 'Remember the Maine!''
Ford, saying, 'History is bunk!'
And Wilson, saying, 'What is good for General Motors –'

Who is it, singing? Don't you hear singing?
It is the dead of Cripple Creek;
Coxey's army
Like turkeys are singing from the tops of trees!
And the Whiskey Boys are drunk outside Philadelphia.

Sleet Storm on the Merritt Parkway

I look out at the white sleet covering the still streets,
As we drive through Scarsdale –
The sleet began falling as we left Connecticut,
And the wet winter leaves swirled in the wet air after cars
Like hands suddenly turned over in a conversation.
Now the frost has nearly buried the short green grass of
  March;

Seeing the sheets of sleet untouched on the wide streets,
I think of the many comfortable homes stretching for miles,
Two and three storeys, solid, with polished floors,
With white curtains in the upstairs bedrooms,
And small perfume flagons of black glass on the window sills,
And warm bathrooms with guest towels, and electric lights –
What a magnificent place for a child to grow up!
And yet the children end in the river of price-fixing,
Or in the snowy field of the insane asylum.
The sleet falls – so many cars moving toward New York –
Last night we argued about the Marines invading Guatemala
    in 1947,
The United Fruit Company had one water spigot for 200
    families,
And the ideals of America, our freedom to criticize,
The slave systems of Rome and Greece, and no one agreed.

Andrew Jackson's Speech

Dido to Aeneas: 'I have broke faith with the ashes of Sichaeus.'

I HEARD Andrew Jackson say, as he closed his Virgil:

'The harsh ravishers in Detroit, inheritors of the soot
   Of chimney boys, when they raised the mighty poor,
   Broke faith with the cinders of Sichaeus.

'I shot to save the honour of my wife;
   And I would shoot again, to save my people.
   The Republic lies in the blossoms of Washington.

'The poor have been raised up by the Revolution.
   Washington, riding in cold snow at Valley Forge,
   Warned the poor never to take another husband.'

His voice rose in the noisy streets of Detroit.

After Lorca
(For M. Marti)

THE church is a business, and the rich
are the business men.
                    When they pull on the bells, the
poor come piling in and when a poor man dies, he has a
    wooden
cross, and they rush through the ceremony.

But when a rich man dies, they
drag out the Sacrament
and a golden Cross, and go *doucement, doucement*
to the cemetery.

And the poor love it
and think it's crazy.

I Know a Man

As I sd to my
friend, because I am
always talking, – John, I

sd, which was not his
name, the darkness sur-
rounds us, what

can we do against
it, or else, shall we &
why not, buy a goddamn big car,

drive, he sd, for
christ's sake, look
out where yr going.

The Hill

IT is sometime since I have been
to what it was had once turned me backwards,
and made my head into
a cruel instrument.

It is simple
to confess. Then done,
to walk away, walk away,
to come again.

But that form, I must answer,
is dead in me, completely,
and I will not allow it
to reappear—

Saith perversity, the wilful,
the magnanimous cruelty,
which is in me
like a hill.

The Signboard

THE quieter the people are
the slower the time passes

until there is a solitary man
sitting in the figure of silence.

Then scream at him,
come here you idiot it's going to go off.

A face that is no face
but the features, of a face, pasted

on a face until that face
is faceless, answers by

a being nothing there
where there was a man.

The Cracks

DON'T step
so lightly. Break
your back, missed
the step. Don't go

away mad, lady in
the nightmare. You
are central,
even necessary.

I will attempt to describe you.
I will be completely without
face, a lost
chance, nothing at all left.

'Well,' he said
as he was leaving,
'blood
tells.'

But you remembered quickly
other times, other faces,
and I slipped between the good
intentions, breathlessly.

What a good boy am I who
wants to. Will you,
mother, come quickly,
won't you. Why not

go quietly, be left
with a memory
or an insinuation or two
of cracks in a pavement.

For Love

(For Bobbie)

YESTERDAY I wanted to
speak of it, that sense above
the others to me
important because all

that I know derives
from what it teaches me.
Today, what is it that
is finally so helpless,

different, despairs of its own
statement, wants to
turn away, endlessly
to turn away.

If the moon did not . . .
no, if you did not
I wouldn't either, but
what would I not

do, what prevention, what
thing so quickly stopped.
That is love yesterday
or tomorrow, not

now. Can I eat
what you give me. I
have not earned it. Must
I think of everything

as earned. Now love also
becomes a reward so
remote from me I have
only made it with my mind.

Here is tedium,
despair, a painful
sense of isolation and
whimsical if pompous

self-regard. But that image
is only of the mind's
vague structure, vague to me
because it is my own.

Love, what do I think
to say. I cannot say it.
What have you become to ask,
what have I made you into,

companion, good company,
crossed legs with skirt, or
soft body under
the bones of the bed.

Nothing says anything
but that which it wishes
would come true, fears
what else might happen in

some other place, some
other time not this one.
A voice in my place, an
echo of that only in yours.

Let me stumble into
not the confession but
the obsession I begin with
now. For you

also (also)
some time beyond place, or
place beyond time, no
mind left to

say anything at all,
that face gone, now.
Into the company of love
it all returns.

Kore

As I was walking
      I came upon
chance walking
      the same road upon.

As I sat down
      by chance to move
later
      if and as I might,

light the wood was,
      light and green,
and what I saw
      before I had not seen.

It was a lady
      accompanied
by goat men
      leading her.

Her hair held earth.
    Her eyes were dark.
A double flute
    made her move.

'O love,
    where are you
leading
    me now?'

The Rain

ALL night the sound had
come back again,
and again falls
this quiet, persistent rain.

What am I to myself
that must be remembered,
insisted upon,
so often? Is it

that never the ease,
even the hardness,
of rain falling
will have for me

something other than this,
something not so insistent-
am I to be locked in this
final uneasiness.

Love, if you love me,
lie next to me.
Be for me, like rain,
the getting out

of the tiredness, the fatuousness, the semi-
lust of intentional indifference.
Be wet
with a decent happiness.

The Power Station

THINK back now to that cleft
In the live rock. A deep voice filled the cave,
Raving up out of cells each time in some way left
Huger and vaguer. There was a kind of nave

Strewn with potsherd and bone,
The tribe's offspring, converted now, rejoice
In our sane god. But, two or three hours south, not known
To them, the charges of the other's voice

Break into light and churn
Through evening fields. Soon a first town is lit,
Is lived in. Grounded. Green. A truth fit to unlearn
The blind delirium that still utters it.

Angel

ABOVE my desk, whirring and self-important
(Though not much larger than a hummingbird)
In finely woven robes, school of Van Eyck,
Hovers an evidently angelic visitor.
He points one index finger out the window
At winter snatching to its heart,
To crystal vacancy, the misty
Exhalations of houses and of people running home
From the cold sun pounding on the sea;
While with the other hand
He indicates the piano
Where the Sarabande No. 1 lies open
At a passage I shall never master

But which has already, and effortlessly mastered me.
He drops his jaw as if to say, or sing,
'Between the world God made
And this music of Satie,
Each glimpsed through veils, but whole,
Radiant and willed,
Demanding praise, demanding surrender,
How can you sit there with your notebook?
What do you think you are doing?'
However he says nothing – wisely: I could mention
Flaws in God's world, or Satie's; and for that matter
How did he come by *his* taste for Satie?
Half to tease him, I turn back to my page,
Its phrases thus far clotted, unconnected.
The tiny angel shakes his head.
There is no smile on his round, hairless face.
He does not want even these few lines written.

Childlessness

THE weather of this winter night, my mistress
Ranting and raining, wakes me. Her cloak blown back
To show the lining's dull lead foil
Sweeps along asphalt. Houses
Look blindly on; one glimmers through a blind.
Outside, I hear her tricklings
Arraign my little plot:
Had it or not agreed
To transplantation for the common good
Of certain rare growths yielding guaranteed
Gold pollen, gender of suns, large, hardy,
Enviable blooms? But in my garden
Nothing is planted. Neither
Is that glimmering window mine.

I lie and think about the rain,
How it has been drawn up from the impure ocean,
From gardens lightly, deliberately tainted;
How it falls back, time after time,
Through poisons visible at sunset
When the enchantress, masked as friend, unfurls
Entire bolts of voluminous pistachio,
Saffron, and rose.
These, as I fall back to sleep,
And other slow colours clothe me, glide
To rest, then burst along my limbs like buds,
Like bombs from the navigator's vantage,
Waking me, lulling me. Later I am shown
The erased metropolis reassembled
On sampans, freighted each
With toddlers, holy dolls, dead ancestors.
One tiny monkey puzzles over fruit.
The vision rises and falls, the garland
Gently takes root
In the sea's coma. Hours go by
Before I can stand to own
A sky stained red, a world
Clad only in rags, threadbare,
Dabbling the highway's ice with blood.
A world. The cloak thrown down for it to wear
In token of past servitude
Has fallen onto the shoulders of my parents
Whom it is eating to the bone.

After Greece

LIGHT into the olive entered
And was oil. Rain made the huge pale stones
Shine from within. The moon turned his hair white
Who next stepped from between the columns,
Shielding his eyes. All through
The countryside were old ideas
Found lying open to the elements.
Of the gods' houses only
A minor premise here and there
Would be balancing the heaven of fixed stars
Upon a Doric capital. The rest
Lay spilled, their fluted drums half sunk in cyclamen
Or deep in water's biting clarity
Which just barely upheld me
The next week, when I sailed for home.
But where is home – these walls?
These limbs? The very spaniel underfoot
Races in sleep, toward what?
It is autumn. I did not invite
Those guests, windy and brittle, who drink my liquor.
Returning from a walk I find
The bottles filled with spleen, my room itself
Smeared by reflection on to the far hemlocks.
I some days flee in dream
Back to the exposed porch of the maidens
Only to find my great-great-grandmothers
Erect there, peering
Into a globe of red Bohemian glass.
As it swells and sinks, I call up
Graces, Furies, Fates, removed
To my country's warm, lit halls, with rivets forced
Through drapery, and nothing left to bear.
They seem anxious to know
What holds up heaven nowadays.

I start explaining how in that vast fire
Were other irons – well, Art, Public Spirit,
Ignorance, Economics, Love of Self,
Hatred of Self, a hundred more,
Each burning to be felt, each dedicated
To sparing us the worst; how I distrust them
As I should have done those ladies; how I want
Essentials: salt, wine, olive, the light, the scream –
No! I have scarcely named you,
And look, in a flash you stand full-grown before me,
Row upon row, Essentials,
Dressed like your sister caryatids
Or tombstone angels jealous of their dead,
With undulant coiffures, lips weathered, cracked by grime,
And faultless eyes gone blank beneath the immense
Zinc and gunmetal northern sky. . . .
Stay then. Perhaps the system
Calls for spirits. This first glass I down
To the last time
I ate and drank in that old world. May I
Also survive its meanings, and my own.

From *Heart's Needle*

I

CHILD of my winter, born
When the new fallen soldiers froze
In Asia's steep ravines and fouled the snows,
When I was torn

By love I could not still,
By fear that silenced my cramped mind
To that cold war where, lost, I could not find
My peace in my will,

All those days we could keep
Your mind a landscape of new snow
Where the chilled tenant-farmer finds, below,
His fields asleep

In their smooth covering, white
As quilts to warm the resting bed
Of birth or pain, spotless as paper spread
For me to write,

And thinks: Here lies my land
Unmarked by agony, the lean foot
Of the weasel tracking, the thick trapper's boot;
And I have planned

My chances to restrain
The torments of demented summer or
Increase the deepening harvest here before
It snows again.

IV

No one can tell you why
the season will not wait;
the night I told you I
must leave, you wept a fearful rate
to stay up late.

Now that it's turning Fall,
we go to take our walk
among municipal
flowers, to steal one off its stalk,
to try and talk.

We huff like windy giants
scattering with our breath
gray-headed dandelions;
Spring is the cold wind's aftermath.
The poet saith.

But the asters, too, are gray,
ghost-gray. Last night's cold
is sending on their way
petunias and dwarf marigold,
hunched sick and old.

Like nerves caught in a graph,
the morning-glory vines
frost has erased by half
still scrawl across their rigid twines.
Like broken lines

of verses I can't make.
In its unravelling loom
we find a flower to take,
with some late buds that might still bloom,
back to your room.

Night comes and the stiff dew.
I'm told a friend's child cried
    because a cricket, who
had minstrelled every night outside
        her window, died.

VI

    Easter has come around
again; the river is rising
    over the thawed ground
and the banksides. When you come you bring
    an egg dyed lavender.
We shout along our bank to hear
our voices returning from the hills to meet us.
We need the landscape to repeat us.

    You lived on this bank first.
While nine months filled your term, we knew
    how your lungs, immersed
in the womb, miraculously grew
    their useless folds till
the fierce, cold air rushed in to fill
them out like bushes thick with leaves. You took your hour,
    caught breath, and cried with your full lung power.

    Over the stagnant bight
we see the hungry bank swallow
    flaunting his free flight
still; we sink in mud to follow
    the killdeer from the grass
that hides her nest. That March there was
rain; the rivers rose; you could hear killdeers flying
    all night over the mudflats crying.

    You bring back how the red-
winged blackbird shrieked, slapping frail wings,
    diving at my head —
I saw where her tough nest, cradled, swings

in tall reeds that must sway
with the winds blowing every way.
If you recall much, you recall this place. You still
live nearby – on the opposite hill.

After the sharp windstorm
of July Fourth, all that summer
through the gentle, warm
afternoons, we heard great chain saws chirr
like iron locusts. Crews
of roughneck boys swarmed to cut loose
branches wrenched in the shattering wind, to hack free
all the torn limbs that could sap the tree.

In the debris lay
starlings, dead. Near the park's birdrun
we surprised one day
a proud, tan-spatted, buff-brown pigeon.
In my hands she flapped so
fearfully that I let her go.
Her keeper came. And we helped snarl her in a net.
You bring things I'd as soon forget.

You raise into my head
a Fall night that I came once more
to sit on your bed;
sweat beads stood out on your arms and fore-
head and you wheezed for breath,
for help, like some child caught beneath
its comfortable woolly blankets, drowning there.
Your lungs caught and would not take the air.

Of all things, only we
have power to choose that we should die;
nothing else is free
in this world to refuse it. Yet I,

who say this, could not raise
myself from bed how many days
to the thieving world. Child, I have another wife,
another child. We try to choose our life.

The Examination

UNDER the thick beams of that swirly smoking light,
    The black robes are clustering, huddled in together.
Hunching their shoulders, they spread short, broad sleeves
    like night-
    Black grackles' wings and reach out bone-yellow leather-

y fingers, each to each. They are prepared. Each turns
    His single eye – or since one can't discern their eyes,
That reflective, single, moon-pale disc which burns
    Over each brow – to watch this uncouth shape that lies

Strapped to their table. One probes with his ragged nails
    The slate-sharp calf, explores the thigh and the lean
    thews
Of the groin. Others raise, red as piratic sails,
    His wing, stretching, trying the pectoral sinews.

One runs his finger down the wheat of that cruel
    Golden beak, lifts back the horny lids from the eyes,
Peers down in one bright eye, malign as a jewel,
    And steps back suddenly, 'He is anaesthetized?'

'He is. He is. Yes. Yes.' The tallest of them, bent
    Down by the head, rises, 'This drug possesses powers
Sufficient to still all gods in this firmament.
    This is Garuda who was fierce. He's yours for hours.'

'We shall continue, please.' Now, once again, he bends
    To the skull, and its clamped tissues. Into the cran-
ial cavity, he plunges both of his hands
    Like obstetric forceps and lifts out the great brain,

Holds it aloft, then gives it to the next who stands
    Beside him. Each, in turn, accepts it, although loath,
Turns it this way, that way, feels it between his hands
    Like a wasps' nest or some sickening outsized growth.

They must decide what thoughts each part of it must think;
    They tap at, then listen beside, each suspect lobe,
Then, with a crow's quill dipped into India ink,
    Mark on its surface, as if on a map or globe,

The dangerous areas which need to be excised.
    They rinse it, then apply antiseptic to it.
And silver saws appear which, inch by inch, slice
    Through its ancient folds and ridges, like thick suet.

It's rinsed, dried, and daubed with thick salves. The smoky
    saws
    Are scrubbed, resterilized, and polished till they gleam.
The brain is repacked in its case. Pinched in their claws,
    Glimmering needles stitch it up, that leave no seam.

Meantime, one of them has set blinders to the eyes,
    Inserted light packing beneath each of the ears
And caulked the nostrils in. One, with thin twine, ties
    The genitals off. With long wooden-handled sheers,

Another chops pinions out of the scarlet wings.
    It's hoped that with disuse he will forget the sky
Or, at least, in time, learn, among other things,
    To fly no higher than his superiors fly.

Well; that's a beginning. The next time, they can split
    His tongue and teach him to talk correctly, can give
Him memory of fine books and choose clothing fit
    For the integrated area where he'll live.

Their candidate may live to give them thanks one day.
　　He will recover and may hope for such success
He shall return to join their ranks. Bowing away,
　　They nod, whispering, 'One of ours; one of ours. Yes.
　　Yes.'

Phi Beta Kappa poem, 1961, Columbia University

Monet: 'Les Nymphéas'

THE eyelids glowing, some chill morning.
O world half-known through opening, twilit lids
　　Before the vague face clenches into light;
O universal waters like a cloud,
　　Like those first clouds of half-created matter;
O all things rising, rising like the fumes
　　From waters falling, O forever falling;
Infinite, the skeletal shells that fall, relinquished,
　　The snowsoft sift of the diatoms, like selves
Downdrifting age upon age through milky oceans;
　　O slow downdrifting of the atoms;
O island nebulae and O the nebulous islands
　　Wandering these mists like falsefires, which are true,
Bobbing like milkweed, like warm lanterns bobbing
　　Through the snowfilled windless air, blinking and passing
As we pass into the memory of women
　　Who are passing. Within those depths
What ravening? What devouring rage?
　　How shall our living know its ends of yielding?
These things have taken me as the mouth an orange —
　　That acrid sweet juice entering every cell;
And I am shared out. I become these things:

166

These lilies, if these things *are* waterlilies
Which are dancers growing dim across no floor;
    These mayflies; whirled dust orbitting in the sun;
This blossoming diffused as rushlights; galactic vapours;
    Fluorescence into which we pass and penetrate;
O soft as the thighs of women;
    O radiance, into which I go on dying. . . .

Hymn

I KNOW if I find you I will have to leave the earth
and go on out
    over the sea marshes and the brant in bays
and over the hills of tall hickory
and over the crater lakes and canyons
and on up through the spheres of diminishing air
past the blackset noctilucent clouds
      where one wants to stop and look
way past all the light diffusions and bombardments
up farther than the loss of sight
    into the unseasonal undifferentiated empty stark

And I know if I find you I will have to stay with the earth
inspecting with thin tools and ground eyes
trusting the microvilli sporangia and simplest coelenterates
and praying for a nerve cell
with all the soul of my chemical reactions
and going right on down where the eye sees only traces

You are everywhere partial and entire
You are on the inside of everything and on the outside

I walk down the path down the hill where the sweetgum
has begun to ooze spring sap at the cut
and I see how the bark cracks and winds like no other bark
chasmal to my ant-soul running up and down
and if I find you I must go out deep into your far
    resolutions
and if I find you I must stay here with the separate leaves

Terrain

THE soul is a region without definite boundaries
    it is not certain a prairie
can exhaust it
    or a range enclose it:
it floats (self-adjusting) like the continental mass.
    where it towers most
extending its deepest mantling base
    (exactly proportional):
does not flow all one way: there is a divide:
    river systems thrown like winter tree-shadows
against the hills: branches, runs, high lakes:
    stagnant lily-marshes:

is variable, has weather: floods unbalancing
    gut it, silt altering the
distribution of weight, the nature of content:
    whirlwinds move through it
or stand spinning like separate orders: the moon comes:
    there are barren spots: bogs, rising
by self-accretion from themselves, a growth into
    destruction of growth,
change of character,
    invasion of peat by poplar and oak: semi-precious
stones and precious metals drop from muddy water into mud:

it is an area of poise, really, held from tipping,
    dark wild water, fierce eels, countercurrents:
a habitat, precise ecology of forms
    mutually to some extent
tolerable, not entirely self-destroying: a crust afloat:
    a scum, foam to the deep and other-natured:
but deeper than depth, too: a vacancy and swirl:

it may be spherical, light and knowledge merely
    the iris and opening

to the dark methods of its sight: how it comes and
    goes, ruptures and heals,
whirls and stands still: the moon comes: terrain

Prospecting

COMING to cottonwoods, an
orange rockshelf,
and in the gully
an edging of stream willows,

I made camp
and turned my mule loose
to graze in the dark
evening of the mountain.

Drowzed over the coals
and my loneliness
like an inner image went
out and shook
hands with the willows,

and running up the black scarp
tugged the heavy moon
up and over into light,

and on a hill-thorn of sage
called with the coyotes
and told ghost stories to
a night circle of lizards.
Tipping on its handle
the Dipper unobtrusively
poured out the night.

At dawn returning, wet
to the hips with meetings,
my loneliness woke me up
and we merged refreshed into
the breaking of camp and day.

Loss

WHEN the sun
falls behind the sumac
thicket the
wild
yellow daisies
in diffuse evening shade
lose their
rigorous attention
and
half-wild with loss
turn
any way the wind does
and lift their
petals up
to float
off their stems
and go

A Supermarket in California

WHAT thoughts I have of you tonight, Walt Whitman, for I walked down the sidestreets under the trees with a headache self-conscious looking at the full moon.

In my hungry fatigue, and shopping for images, I went into the neon fruit supermarket, dreaming of your enumerations!

What peaches and what penumbras! Whole families shopping at night! Aisles full of husbands! Wives in the avocados, babies in the tomatoes! – and you, Garcia Lorca, what were you doing down by the watermelons?

I saw you, Walt Whitman, childless, lonely old grubber, poking among the meats in the refrigerator and eyeing the grocery boys.

I heard you asking questions of each: Who killed the pork chops? What price bananas? Are you my Angel?

I wandered in and out of the brilliant stacks of cans following you, and followed in my imagination by the store detective.

We strode down the open corridors together in our solitary fancy tasting artichokes, possessing every frozen delicacy, and never passing the cashier.

Where are we going, Walt Whitman? The doors close in an hour. Which way does your beard point tonight?

(I touch your book and dream of our odyssey in the supermarket and feel absurd.)

Will we walk all night through solitary streets? The trees add shade to shade, lights out in the houses, we'll both be lonely.

Will we stroll dreaming of the lost America of love past
blue automobiles in driveways, home to our silent cottage?

Ah, dear father, graybeard, lonely old courage-teacher,
what America did you have when Charon quit poling his
ferry and you got out on a smoking bank and stood watching
the boat disappear on the black waters of Lethe?

Berkeley 1955

Dream Record: June 8 1955

A DRUNKEN night in my house with a
boy, San Francisco: I lay asleep:
darkness:
          I went back to Mexico City
and saw Joan Burroughs leaning
forward in a garden-chair, arms
on her knees. She studied me with
clear eyes and downcast smile, her
face restored to a fine beauty
tequila and salt had made strange
before the bullet in her brow.

We talked of the life since then.
Well, what's Burroughs doing now?
Bill on earth, he's in North Africa.
Oh, and Kerouac? Jack still jumps
with the same beat genius as before,
notebooks filled with Buddha.
I hope he makes it, she laughed.
Is Huncke still in the can? No,
last time I saw him on Times Square.
And how is Kenney? Married, drunk
and golden in the East. You? New
loves in the West—

                    Then I knew
she was a dream: and questioned her
– Joan, what kind of knowledge have
the dead? can you still love
your mortal acquaintances?
What do you remember of us?

                              She
faded in front of me – The next instant
I saw her rain-stained tombstone
rear an illegible epitaph
under the gnarled branch of a small
tree in the wild grass
of an unvisited garden in Mexico.

To Lindsay

VACHEL, the stars are out
dusk has fallen on the Colorado road
a car crawls slowly across the plain
in the dim light the radio blares its jazz
the heartbroken salesman lights another cigarette
In another city 27 years ago
I see your shadow on the wall
you're sitting in your suspenders on the bed
the shadow hand lifts up a pistol to your head
your shade falls over on the floor

                              Paris 1958

Message

SINCE we had changed
rogered spun worked
wept and pissed together
I wake up in the morning
with a dream in my eyes
but you are gone in N Y
remembering me Good
I love you I love you
& your brothers are crazy
I accept their drunk cases
It's too long that I have been alone
it's too long that I've sat up in bed
without anyone to touch on the knee, man
or woman I don't care what anymore, I
want love I was born for I want you with me now
Ocean liners boiling over the Atlantic
Delicate steelwork of unfinished skyscrapers
Back end of the dirigible roaring over Lakehurst
Six women dancing together on a red stage naked
The leaves are green on all the trees in Paris now
I will be home in two months and look you in the eyes

1958

The End

I AM I, old Father Fisheye that begat the ocean, the worm
at my own ear, the serpent turning around a tree,
I sit in the mind of the oak and hide in the rose, I know if any
wake up, none but my death,
come to me bodies, come to me prophecies, come all fore-
boding, come spirits and visions,
I receive all, I'll die of cancer, I enter the coffin forever, I
close my eye, I disappear,
I fall on myself in winter snow, I roll in a great wheel through
rain, I watch fuckers in convulsion,
car screech, furies groaning their basso music, memory fading
in the brain, men imitating dogs,
I delight in a woman's belly, youth stretching his breasts and
thighs to sex, the cock sprung inward
gassing its seed on the lips of Yin, the beasts dance in Siam,
they sing opera in Moscow,
my boys yearn at dusk on stoops, I enter New York, I play
my jazz on a Chicago Harpsichord,
Love that bore me I bear back to my Origin with no loss, I
float over the vomiter
thrilled with my deathlessness, thrilled with this endlessness I
dice and bury,
come Poet shut up eat my word, and taste my mouth in your
ear.

N.Y. 1960

First Party at Ken Keseys with Hell's Angels

COOL black night thru redwoods
cars parked outside in shade
behind the gate, stars dim above
the ravine, a fire burning by the side
porch and a few tired souls hunched over
in black leather jackets. In the huge
wooden house, a yellow chandelier
at 3 a.m. the blast of loudspeakers
hi-fi Rolling Stones Ray Charles Beatles
Jumping Joe Jackson and twenty youths
dancing to the vibration thru the floor,
a little weed in the bathroom, girls in scarlet
tights, one muscular smooth skinned man
sweating dancing for hours, beer cans
bent littering the yard, a hanged man
sculpture dangling from a high creek branch,
children sleeping softly in bedroom bunks,
And 4 police cars parked outside the painted
gate, red lights revolving in the leaves.

December 1965

Lie Closed, My Lately Loved

LIE closed, my lately loved, in the far bed
At the foot of the moon, barred by sash and shade.
Now your eyes are shells adrift in shadow,
The fires banked. Under the furled sheets,
The long sloop of your body swings about
The anchor of a dream. The dark applause
Of leaves wakes in the wind the ear makes
When it hears no wind; the sapling bows
Against the wall in the footlight of the moon.

One hour away from sweating animals,
Afraid to wake the children or themselves,
We're locked apart, though something of your shape
Still molds my hand. I breathe you still.
I breathe the gross, the delicate, together.
I build a vision from our mingled dreams.
A heavy stallion rumbles in the straw,
The stud for all the trembling mares. Around
His yellow mouth hang crumbs of flowers.

What Do You Do When It's Spring?

WHAT do you do when it's spring?
I mean what do you do when it's really green
Not just in the private parts of the links
But even between the rusting tracks
Where the dead train slipped under the fence
Into the dead factory?

What would you tell
Your wife if you woke with a green thumb
And everything you touched turned to grass?
And you still owed six payments on winter?

What would you do with a bird
So small it could swim in and out
Through the bars of its song?

What do you do when a fine green spring
Sifts through the antenna
And the records run like demented aspirin
Through the wire services? It happens.
Don't kid yourself.

What do you say when you can't find your camera
And miss something beautiful, your neighbor's wife
Opening at the seams, or the march
Of the red tricycles on the fire stations,
Or the pedlar who is not running a survey
In your neighborhood.

What would you say if the garbage man
Cast off his mask of oranges and red
Butcher's paper and danced between your very eyes
The pure dance of a person becoming himself.
Or if the meter man had a name.
Or if the milkman led up your green driveway
A buxom cow, spraying sweet milk and clover
Wearing a milking machine like curlers
On her horns?

Or if the mailman took root in your box,
Shedding green news, and mailing himself
Over and over again, in to the sprinkling evening?

What do you think when you feel
That the Great God Ampersand links flowers and ceramics,
Table salt and Triton, or rocks like a treble clef
Beneath the rusted swing and slide?

I mean before schools and jails open.
I mean before the paper knocks at the railing.
I mean before the rose vine lost its legs.

What do you do when you're born?

Looking Both Ways Before Crossing

I

ON A day when smoke lies down in alleys,
when a football skitters from behind the parish house,
when a faint bitterness in wines and ciders
curls a moment at the back of the tongue,
I find myself again
an unfrocked minister of change,
looking both ways before crossing.

I set out for the instant,
telling the wind to stop in the trees.
But leaf fires leap into the ash and air,
or sing back along the limb
where the sun picks for its eye
one drop on a leaf.

I am more leaf than tree.
Wind moves its wave forms through my flesh,
time falls from the back of mirrors,
where, through my eyes,
I see the child and skull.

II

How easy to see an old town as a ship,
with a bow wave of junked cars and chickencoops
plowing with a full spread of elm through grain.

Young men are swimming for their lives,
while their elders become their own potatoes,
holding their thick, broken hands
in the stained light of the church.
Outside, the corn rasps,
black and venereal,
rising from the bones of planters.

What earth can I leave
that does not take me back
under the harsh corn?

III

Who named me tenant of change?
Why must I chronicle the last places?
Lost riverbeds, closing under willows,
broken wings of kites,
glints of transits
across the valley.

The old hotel shrinks in a desert of parking meters.
What can it say:
drummers, revivalists swollen like a tent,
horse traders?
No, they're tying off the tubes in the basement,
the plumbing has hot flashes,
the walls strip down their paint.
The shaker slows,
and the barkeep fades into the mirror.

IV

I am old enough to be my own father,
and yet the green tongue of spring
stirs me like a child.
In the first yeast of April
I rise to the taut blue of kites,

leaned out over the healing town.
In the young faces of girls,
beauty turns to me
like sudden flowers.

Why must I be father and son,
hating and loving across years?
I want to take my own hand,
and in a still place in the wind,
be what I have become.

Why I am not a Painter

I AM not a painter, I am a poet.
Why? I think I would rather be
a painter, but I am not. Well,

For instance, Mike Goldberg
is starting a painting. I drop in.
'Sit down and have drink' he
says. I drink; we drink. I look
up. 'You have SARDINES in it.'
'Yes, it needed something there.'
'Oh,' I go and the days go by
and I drop in again. The painting
is going on, and I go, and the days
go by. I drop in. The painting is
finished. 'Where's SARDINES?'
All that's left is just
letters, 'It was too much,' Mike says.

But me? One day I am thinking of
a color: orange. I write a line
about orange. Pretty soon it is a
whole page of words, not lines.
Then another page. There should be
so much more, not of orange, of
words, of how terrible orange is
and life. Days go by. It is even in
prose, I am a real poet. My poem
is finished and I haven't mentioned
orange yet. It's twelve poems, I call
it ORANGES. And one day in a gallery
I see Mike's painting, called SARDINES.

1956

A Step Away from Them

Iт's my lunch hour, so I go
for a walk among the hum-colored
cabs. First, down the sidewalk
where laborers feed their dirty
glistening torsos sandwiches
and Coca-Cola, with yellow helmets
on. They protect them from falling
bricks, I guess. Then onto the
avenue where skirts are flipping
above heels and blow up over
grates. The sun is hot, but the
cabs stir up the air. I look
at bargains in wristwatches. There
are cats playing in sawdust.

                                    On
to Times Square, where the sign
blows smoke over my head, and higher
the waterfall pours lightly. A
Negro stands in a doorway with a
toothpick, languorously agitating.
A blonde chorus girl clicks: he
smiles and rubs his chin. Everything
suddenly honks: it is 12:40 of
a Thursday.
                    Neon in daylight is a
great pleasure, as Edwin Denby would
write, as are light bulbs in daylight.
I stop for a cheeseburger at JULIET'S
CORNER. Giulietta Masina, wife of
Federico Fellini, *è bell' attrice.*
And chocolate malted. A lady in
foxes on such a day puts her poodle
in a cab.

There are several Puerto
Ricans on the avenue today, which
makes it beautiful and warm. First
Bunny died, then John Latouche,
then Jackson Pollock. But is the
earth as full as life was full, of them?
And one has eaten and one walks,
past the magazines with nudes
and the posters for BULLFIGHT and
the Manhattan Storage Warehouse,
which they'll soon tear down. I
used to think they had the Armory
Show there.
A glass of papaya juice
and back to work. My heart is in my
pocket, it is Poems by Pierre Reverdy.

1956

Steps

How funny you are today New York
like Ginger Rogers in *Swingtime*
and St Bridget's steeple leaning a little to the left

here I have just jumped out of a bed full of V-days
(I got tired of D-days) and blue you there still
accepts me foolish and free
all I want is a room up there
and you in it
and even the traffic halt so thick is a way
for people to rub up against each other
and when their surgical appliances lock
they stay together
for the rest of the day (what a day)
I go by to check a slide and I say
that painting's not so blue

185

where's Lana Turner
she's out eating
and Garbo's backstage at the Met
everyone's taking their coat off
so they can show a rib-cage to the rib-watchers
and the park's full of dancers with their tights and shoes
in little bags
who are often mistaken for worker-outers at the West Side Y
why not
the Pittsburgh Pirates shout because they won
and in a sense we're all winning
we're alive

the apartment was vacated by a gay couple
who moved to the country for fun
they moved a day too soon
even the stabbings are helping the population explosion
though in the wrong country
and all those liars have left the UN
the Seagram Building's no longer rivalled in interest
not that we need liquor (we just like it)

and the little box is out on the sidewalk
next to the delicatessen
so the old man can sit on it and drink beer
and get knocked off it by his wife later in the day
while the sun is still shining

oh god it's wonderful
to get out of bed
and drink too much coffee
and smoke too many cigarettes
and love you so much

1961

Some Trees

THESE are amazing: each
Joining a neighbour, as though speech
Were a still performance.
Arranging by chance

To meet as far this morning
From the world as agreeing
With it, you and I
Are suddenly what the trees try

To tell us we are:
That their merely being there
Means something; that soon
We may touch, love, explain.

And glad not to have invented
Such comeliness, we are surrounded:
A silence already filled with noises,
A canvas on which emerges

A chorus of smiles, a winter morning.
Placed in a puzzling light, and moving,
Our days put on such reticence
These accents seem their own defence.

The Picture of Little J. A. in a Prospect of Flowers

*'He was spoilt from childhood by the future, which he mastered
rather early and apparently without great difficulty'*
BORIS PASTERNAK

I

DARKNESS falls like a wet sponge
And Dick gives Genevieve a swift punch
In the pyjamas. 'Aroint thee, witch.'
Her tongue from previous ecstasy
Releases thoughts like little hats.

'He clap'd me first during the eclipse.
Afterwards I noted his manner
Much altered. But he sending
At that time certain handsome jewels
I durst not seem to take offence.'

In a far recess of summer
Monks are playing soccer.

II

So far is goodness a mere memory
Or naming of recent scenes of badness
That even these lives, children,
You may pass through to be blessed,
So fair does each invent his virtue.

And coming from a white world, music
Will sparkle at the lips of many who are
Beloved. Then these, as dirty handmaidens
To some transparent witch, will dream
Of a white hero's subtle wooing,
And time shall force a gift on each.

That beggar to whom you gave no cent
Striped the night with his strange descant.

III

Yet I cannot escape the picture
Of my small self in that bank of flowers:
My head among the blazing phlox
Seemed a pale and gigantic fungus.
I had a hard stare, accepting

Everything, taking nothing,
As though the rolled-up future might stink
As loud as stood the sick moment
The shutter clicked. Though I was wrong,
Still, as the loveliest feelings

Must soon find words, and these, yes,
Displace them, so I am not wrong
In calling this comic version of myself
The true one. For as change is horror,
Virtue is really stubbornness

And only in the light of lost words
Can we imagine our rewards.

A Vase of Flowers

THE vase is white and would be a cylinder
If a cylinder were wider at the top than at the bottom.
The flowers are red, white and blue.

All contact with the flowers is forbidden.

The white flowers strain upward
Into a pallid air of their references,
Pushed slightly by the red and blue flowers.

If you were going to be jealous of the flowers,
Please forget it.
They mean absolutely nothing to me.

Thoughts of a Young Girl

'It is such a beautiful day I had to write you a letter
From the tower, and to show I'm not mad:
I only slipped on the cake of soap of the air
And drowned in the bathtub of the world.
You were too good to cry much over me.
And now I let you go. Signed, The Dwarf.'

I passed by late in the afternoon
And the smile still played about her lips
As it has for centuries. She always knows
How to be utterly delightful. Oh my daughter,
My sweetheart, daughter of my late employer, princess,
May you not be long on the way!

Our Youth

Of bricks ... Who built it? Like some crazy balloon
When love leans on us
Its nights ... The velvety pavement sticks to our feet.
The dead puppies turn us back on love.

Where we are. Sometimes
The brick arches led to a room like a bubble, that broke when
  you entered it
And sometimes to a fallen leaf.
We got crazy with emotion, showing how much we knew.

The Arabs took us. We knew
The dead horses. We were discovering coffee,
How it is to be drunk hot, with bare feet
In Canada. And the immortal music of Chopin

Which we had been discovering for several months
Since we were fourteen years old. And coffee grounds,
And the wonder of hands, and the wonder of the day
When the child discovers her first dead hand.

Do you know it? Hasn't she
Observed you too? Haven't you been observed to her?
My, haven't the flowers been? Is the evil
In't? What window? What did you say there?

Heh? Eh? Our youth is dead.
From the minute we discover it with eyes closed
Advancing into mountain light.
Ouch . . . You will never have that young boy,

That boy with the monocle
Could have been your father
He is passing by. No, that other one,
Upstairs. He is the one who wanted to see you.

He is dead. Green and yellow handkerchiefs cover him.
Perhaps he will never rot, I see
That my clothes are dry. I will go.
The naked girl crosses the street.

Blue hampers . . . Explosions,
Ice . . . The ridiculous
Vases of porphyry. All that our youth
Can't use, that it was created for.

It's true we have not avoided our destiny
By weeding out the old people.
Our faces have filled with smoke. We escape
Down the cloud ladder, but the problem has not been solved.

The Young Prince and the Young Princess

THE grass cuts our feet as we wend our way
Across the meadow – you, a child of thirteen
In a man's business suit far too big for you
A symbol of how long we have been together.

I pick the berries for us to eat
Into a tin can and set it on a stump
Soon or late, lateness comes.
Crows come up out of the west.

I want you to examine this solid block of darkness
In which we are imprisoned. But you say, No,
You are tired. You turn over and sleep.
And I sleep, but in my sleep I hear horses carrying you away.

When the breeze is finished it is morning
Again. Wake up. It is time to start walking
Into the heavenly wilderness. This morning, strangers
Come down to the road to feed us. They are afraid to have
    us come so far.

Night comes, but this time it is a different one.
Your feet scarcely seem to touch the grass
As you walk; you have confidence in me;
Moths bump my incandescent head

And I hear the wind. And so it goes. Some day
We will wake up, having fallen in the night
From a high cliff into the white, precious sky.
You will say, 'That is how we lived, you and I.'

From *The Avenue Bearing the Initial
of Christ into the New World*

II

THE fishmarket closed, the fishes gone into flesh.
The smelts draped on each other, fat with roe,
The marble cod hacked into chunks on the counter,
Butterfishes mouths still open, still trying to eat,
Porgies with receding jaws hinged apart
In a grimace of dejection, as if like cows
They had died under the sledgehammer, perches
In grass-green armour, spotted squeteagues
In the melting ice meek-faced and croaking no more,
Mud-eating mullets buried in crushed ice,
Tilefishes with scales like chickenfat,
Spanish mackerels, buttercups on the flanks,
Pot-bellied pikes, two-tone flounders
After the long contortion of pushing both eyes
To the brown side that they might look up,
Lying brown side down, like a mass laying-on of hands,
Or the oath-taking of an army.

The only things alive are the carp
That drift in the black tank in the rear,
Kept living for the usual reason, that they have not died,
And perhaps because the last meal was garbage and they
     might begin stinking
On dying, before the customer was halfway home.
They nudge each other, to be netted,
The sweet flesh to be lifted thrashing in the air,
To be slugged, and then to keep on living
While they are opened on the counter.

Fishes do not die exactly, it is more
That they go out of themselves, the visible part
Remains the same, there is little pallor,
Only the cataracted eyes which have not shut ever
Must look through the mist which crazed Homer.

These are the vegetables of the deep,
The Sheol-flowers of darkness, swimmers
Of denser darknesses where the sun's rays bend for the last
     time
And in the sky there burns this shifty jellyfish
That degenerates and flashes and re-forms.

Motes in the eye land is the lid of,
They are plucked out of the green skim milk of the eye.

Fishes are nailed on the wood,
The big Jew stands like Christ, nailing them to the wood,
He scrapes the knife up the grain, the scales fly,
He unnails them, reverses them, nails them again,
Scrapes and the scales fly. He lops off the heads,
Shakes out the guts as if they did not belong in the first
     place,
And they are flesh for the first time in their lives.

Dear Frau —:
     Your husband, —, died in the Camp Hospital on —. May
I express my sincere sympathy on your bereavement. — was
admitted to the Hospital on — with severe symptoms of ex-
haustion, complaining of difficulties in breathing and pains
in the chest. Despite competent medication and devoted
medical attention, it proved impossible, unfortunately, to
keep the patient alive. The deceased voiced no final requests.

                                        Camp Commandant, —

On 5th Street Bunko Certified Embalmer Catholic
Leans in his doorway drawing on a Natural Bloom Cigar.
He looks up the street. Even the Puerto Ricans are Jews
And the Chinese Laundry closes on Saturday.

Flower-herding Pictures on
Mount Monadnock

I

I CAN support it no longer.
Laughing ruefully at myself
For all I claim to have suffered
I get up. Damned nightmarer!

It is New Hampshire out here,
It is nearly the dawn.
The song of the whipoorwill stops
And the dimension of depth seizes everything.

II

The song of a peabody-bird goes overhead
Like a needle pushed five times through the air.
It enters the leaves, and comes out little changed.

The air is so still
That as they go off through the trees
The love-songs of birds do not get any fainter.

III

The last memory I have
Is of a flower which cannot be touched,

Through the bloom of which, all day,
Fly crazed, missing bees.

IV

As I climb, sweat gets up my nostrils;
For an instant I think I am at the sea.

One summer off Cap Ferrat we watched a black seagull
Straining towards the dawn, we stood in the surf —

Grasshoppers splash up where I step,
The mountain-laurel crashes at my thighs.

V

There is something joyous in the elegies
Of birds. They seem
Caught up in a formal delight,
Though the mourning dove whistles of despair.

But at last in the thousand elegies
The dead rise in our hearts;
On the brink of our happiness we stop
Like someone on a drunk starting to weep.

VI

I kneel at a pool, I look through my face
At the bacteria I think I see crawling through the moss.

My face sees me, the water stirs, the face,
Looking preoccupied, gets knocked from its bones.

VII

I weighed eleven pounds
At birth, having stayed on
Two extra weeks in the womb.
Tempted by room and fresh air,
I came out big as a policeman,
Blue-faced, with narrow red eyes.
It was eight days before the doctor
Would scare my mother with me.

Turning and craning in the vines,
I can make out through the leaves
The old, shimmering nothingness, the sky.

VIII

Green, scaly moosewoods ascend,
Tenants of the shaken paradise.

At every wind, last night's rain
Comes splattering from the leaves.

It drops in flurries, and lies there,
Like footsteps of some running start.

IX

From a rock, a waterfall,
A single trickle like a strand of wire,
Breaks into beads halfway down.

I know the birds fly off,
But the hug of the earth wraps
With moss their graves and the giant boulders.

X

In the forest I discover a flower.

The invisible life of the thing
Goes up in flames that are invisible,
Like cellophane burning in the sunlight.

It burns up. Its drift is to be nothing.

In its covertness it has a way
Of uttering itself in place of itself,
Its blossoms claim to float in the Empyrean,

A wrathful presence on the blur of the ground.

The appeal to heaven breaks off.
The petals begin to fall, in self-forgiveness.
It is a flower. On this mountainside it is dying.

Leviathan

THIS is the black sea-brute bulling through wave-wrack,
Ancient as ocean's shifting hills, who in sea-toils
Travelling, who furrowing the salt acres
Heavily, his wake hoary behind him,
Shoulders spouting, the fist of his forehead
Over wastes grey-green crashing, among horses unbroken
From bellowing fields, past bone-wreck of vessels,
Tide-ruin, wash of lost bodies bobbing
No longer sought for, and islands of ice gleaming,
Who ravening the rank flood, wave-marshalling,
Overmastering the dark sea-marches, finds home
And harvest. Frightening to foolhardiest
Mariners, his size were difficult to describe:
The hulk of him is like hills heaving,
Dark, yet as crags of drift-ice, crowns cracking in thunder,
Like land's self by night black-looming, surf churning and
    trailing
Along his shores' rushing, shoal-water boding
About the dark of his jaws; and who should moor at his edge
And fare on afoot would find gates of no gardens,
But the hill of dark underfoot diving,
Closing overhead, the cold deep, and drowning.
He is called Leviathan, and named for rolling,
First created he was of all creatures,
He has held Jonah three days and nights,
He is that curling serpent that in ocean is,
Sea-fright he is, and the shadow under the earth.
Days there are, nonetheless, when he lies
Like an angel, although a lost angel
On the waste's unease, no eye of man moving,

Bird hovering, fish flashing, creature whatever
Who after him came to herit earth's emptiness.
Froth at flanks seething soothes to stillness,
Waits; with one eye he watches
Dark of night sinking last, with one eye dayrise
As at first over foaming pastures. He makes no cry
Though that light is a breath. The sea curling,
Star-climbed, wind-combed, cumbered with itself still
As at first it was, is the hand not yet contented
Of the Creator. And he waits for the world to begin.

Low Fields and Light

I THINK it is in Virginia, that place
That lies across the eye of my mind now
Like a grey blade set to the moon's roundness,
Like a plain of glass touching all there is.

The flat fields run out to the sea there.
There is no sand, no line. It is autumn.
The bare fields, dark between fences, run
Out to the idle gleam of the flat water.

And the fences go on out, sinking slowly,
With a cow-bird half-way, on a stunted post, watching
How the light slides through them easy as weeds
Or wind, slides over them away out near the sky.

Because even a bird can remember
The fields that were there before the slow
Spread and wash of the edging light crawled
There and covered them, a little more each year.

My father never ploughed there, nor my mother
Waited, and never knowingly I stood there
Hearing the seepage slow as growth, nor knew
When the taste of salt took over the ground.

But you would think the fields were something
To me, so long I stare out, looking
For their shapes or shadows through the matted gleam,
    seeing
Neither what is nor what was, but the flat light rising.

The Bones

It takes a long time to hear what the sands
Seem to be saying, with the wind nudging them,
And then you cannot put it in words nor tell
Why these things should have a voice. All kinds
Of objects come in over the tide-wastes
In the course of a year, with a throaty
Rattle: weeds, driftwood, the bodies of birds
And of fish, shells. For years I had hardly
Considered shells as being bones, maybe
Because of the sound they could still make, though
I knew a man once who could raise a kind
Of wailing tune out of a flute he had,
Made from a fibula: it was much the same
Register as the shells'; the tune did not
Go on when his breath stopped, though you thought it
    would.
Then that morning, coming on the wreck,
I saw the kinship. No recent disaster
But an old ghost from under a green buoy,
Brought in by the last storm, or one from which
The big wind had peeled back the sand grave
To show what was still left: the bleached, chewed-off
Timbers like the ribs of a man or the jaw-bone
Of some extinct beast. Far down the sands its
Broken cage leaned out, casting no shadow
In the veiled light. There was a man sitting beside it
Eating out of a paper, littering the beach

With the bones of a few more fish, while the hulk
Cupped its empty hand high over him. Only he
And I had come to those sands knowing
That they were there. The rest was bones, whatever
Tunes they made. The bones of things; and of men too
And of man's endeavours whose ribs he had set
Between himself and the shapeless tides. Then
I saw how the sand was shifting like water,
That once could walk. Shells were to shut out the sea,
The bones of birds were built for floating
On air and water, and those of fish were devised
For their feeding depths, while a man's bones were framed
For what? For knowing the sands are here,
And coming to hear them a long time; for giving
Shapes to the sprawled sea, weight to its winds,
And wrecks to plead for its sands. These things are not
Limitless: we know there is somewhere
An end to them, though every way you look
They extend farther than a man can see.

Small Woman on Swallow Street

FOUR feet up, under the bruise-blue
Fingered hat-felt, the eyes begin. The sly brim
Slips over the sky, street after street, and nobody
Knows, to stop it. It will cover
The whole world, if there is time. Fifty years'
Start in grey the eyes have; you will never
Catch up to where they are, too clever
And always walking, the legs not long but
The boots big with wide smiles of darkness
Going round and round at their tops, climbing.
They are almost to the knees already, where
There should have been ankles to stop them.

So you must keep walking all the time, hurry, for
The black sea is down where the toes are
And swallows and swallows all. A big coat
Can help save you. But eyes push you down; never
Meet eyes. There are hands in hands, and love
Follows its furs into shut doors; who
Shall be killed first? Do not look up there:
The wind is blowing the building-tops, and a hand
Is sneaking the whole sky another way, but
It will not escape. Do not look up. God is
On High. He can see you. You will die.

Grandfather in the Old Men's Home

GENTLE at last, and as clean as ever,
He did not even need drink any more,
And his good sons unbent and brought him
Tobacco to chew, both times when they came
To be satisfied he was well cared for.
And he smiled all the time to remember
Grandmother, his wife, wearing the true faith
Like an iron nightgown, yet brought to birth
Seven times and raising the family
Through her needle's eye while he got away
Down the green river, finding directions
For boats. And himself coming home sometimes
Well-heeled but blind drunk, to hide all the bread
And shoot holes in the bucket while he made
His daughters pump. Still smiled as kindly in
His sleep beside the other clean old men
To see Grandmother, every night the same,
Huge in her age, with her thumbed-down mouth, come
Hating the river, filling with her stare
His gliding dream, while he turned to water,

While the children they both had begotten,
With old faces now, but themselves shrunken
To child-size again, stood ranged at her side,
Beating their little Bibles till he died.

Views from the High Camp

In the afternoon, while the wind
Lies down in its halcyon self,
A finger of darkness moving like an oar
Follows me through the blinding fields; in the focus
Of its peculiar radiance I have found
Treasures I did not know I had lost, several
Perhaps still in the future. Among them
This epitaph for someone:

Discoverer of absences, beloved lamp,
You that wait,
I have migrated from these footsteps,
I, alone, my own sole generation.

Later, loss will wake like the drowsing birds
And have no word. Here we have watched
The great yellow days turning their spokes
Toward autumn and departure
Through month after month of drought, while daily
The sun has hoisted a long cloud of decision
And hung it in my sight at no distance, in the form
Of a tent full of wind, each cord wrenched in turn.

Be assured that the rain will be released
When it is too late to save the harvest.

Departure's Girl-friend

LONELINESS leapt in the mirrors, but all week
I kept them covered like cages. Then I thought
Of a better thing.

And though it was late night in the city
There I was on my way
To my boat, feeling good to be going, hugging
This big wreath with the words like real
Silver: *Bon Voyage.*

            The night
Was mine but everyone's, like a birthday.
Its fur touched my face in passing. I was going
Down to my boat, my boat,
To see it off, and glad at the thought.
Some leaves of the wreath were holding my hands
And the rest waved good-bye as I walked, as though
They were still alive.

And all went well till I came to the wharf, and no one.

I say no one, but I mean
There was this young man, maybe
Out of the merchant marine,
In some uniform, and I knew who he was; just the same
When he said to me where do you think you're going,
I was happy to tell him.

But he said to me, it isn't your boat,
You don't have one. I said, it's mine, I can prove it:
Look at this wreath, I'm carrying to it,
Bon Voyage. He said, This is the stone wharf, lady,
You don't own anything here.

And as I
Was turning away, the injustice of it
Lit up the buildings, and there I was
In the other and hated city
Where I was born, where nothing is moored, where
The lights crawl over the stone like flies, spelling now,
Now, and the same fat chances roll
Their many eyes; and I step once more
Through a hoop of tears and walk on, holding this
Buoy of flowers in front of my beauty,
Wishing myself the good voyage.

A Gesture by a Lady with an Assumed Name

LETTERS she left to clutter up the desk
Burned in the general gutter when the maid
Came in to do the room and take the risk
Of slipping off the necklace round her head.

Laundry she left to clutter up the floor
Hung to rachitic skeletons of girls
Who worked the bars or laboured up the stair
To crown her blowsy ribbons on their curls.

Lovers she left to clutter up the town
Mourned in the chilly morgue and went away,
All but the husbands sneaking up and down
The stairs of that apartment house all day.

What were they looking for? The cold pretence
Of lamentation offered in a stew?
A note? A gift? A shred of evidence
To love when there was nothing else to do?

Or did they rise to weep for that unheard-
Of love, whose misery cries and does not care
Whether or not the madam hears a word
Or skinny children watch the trodden stair?

Whether or not, how could she love so many,
Then turn away to die as though for none?
I saw the last offer a child a penny
To creep outside and see the cops were gone.

At Thomas Hardy's Birthplace, 1953

I

THE nurse carried him up the stair
Into his mother's sleeping room.
The beeches lashed the roof and dragged the air
    Because of storm.

Wind could have overturned the dead.
Moth and beetle and housefly crept
Under the door to find the lamp, and cowered:
    But still he slept.

The ache and sorrow of darkened earth
Left pathways soft and meadows sodden;
The small Frome overflowed the firth,
    And he lay hidden

In the arms of the tall woman gone
To soothe his mother during the dark;
Nestled against the awkward flesh and bone
    When the rain broke.

II

Last night at Stinsford where his heart
Is buried now, the rain came down.
Cold to the hidden joy, the secret hurt,
    His heart is stone.

But over the dead leaves in the wet
The mouse goes snooping, and the bird.
Something the voiceless earth does not forget
    They come to guard,

Maybe, the heart who would not tell
Whatever secret he learned from the ground,
Who turned aside and heard the human wail,
    That other sound.

More likely, though, the labouring feet
Of fieldmouse, hedgehog, moth and hawk
Seek in the storm what comfort they can get
    Under the rock   .

Where surely the heart will not wake again
To endure the unending beat of the air,
Having been nursed beyond the sopping rain,
    Back down the stair.

Saint Judas

WHEN I went out to kill myself, I caught
A pack of hoodlums beating up a man.
Running to spare his suffering, I forgot
My name, my number, how my day began,
How soldiers milled around the garden stone
And sang amusing songs; how all that day
Their javelins measured crowds; how I alone
Bargained the proper coins, and slipped away.

Banished from heaven, I found this victim beaten,
Stripped, kneed, and left to cry. Dropping my rope
Aside, I ran, ignored the uniforms:
Then I remembered bread my flesh had eaten,
The kiss that ate my flesh. Flayed without hope,
I held the man for nothing in my arms.

Confession to J. Edgar Hoover

HIDING in the church of an abandoned stone,
A Negro soldier
Is flipping the pages of the Articles of War,
That he can't read.

Our father,
Last evening I devoured the wing
Of a cloud.
And, in the city, I sneaked down
To pray with a sick tree.

I labor to die, father,
I ride the great stones,
I hide under stars and maples,
And yet I cannot find my own face.
In the mountains of blast furnaces,
The trees turn their backs on me.

Father, the dark moths
Crouch at the sills of earth, waiting.

And I am afraid of my own prayers.
Father, forgive me.
I did not know what I was doing.

Lying in a Hammock at William Duffy's Farm in Pine Island, Minnesota

OVER my head, I see the bronze butterfly,
Asleep on the black trunk,
Blowing like a leaf in green shadow.
Down the ravine behind the empty house,
The cowbells follow one another
Into the distances of the afternoon.
To my right,
In a field of sunlight between two pines,
The droppings of last year's horses
Blaze into golden stones.
I lean back, as the evening darkens and comes on.
A chicken-hawk floats over, looking for home.
I have wasted my life.

Depressed by a Book of Bad Poetry, I Walk toward an Unused Pasture and Invite the Insects to Join Me

RELIEVED, I let the book fall behind a stone.
I climb a slight rise of grass.
I do not want to disturb the ants
Who are walking single file up the fence post,
Carrying small white petals,
Casting shadows so frail that I can see through them.
I close my eyes for a moment, and listen.
The old grasshoppers
Are tired, they leap heavily now,
Their thighs are burdened.
I want to hear them, they have clear sounds to make.
They have gone to sleep.
Then lovely, far off, a dark cricket begins
In the castles of maple.

The Blessing

JUST off the highway to Rochester, Minnesota,
Twilight bounds softly forth on the grass.
And the eyes of those two Indian ponies
Darken with kindness.
They have come gladly out of the willows
To welcome my friend and me.
We step over the barbed wire into the pasture
Where they have been grazing all day, alone.
They ripple tensely, they can hardly contain their happiness
That we have come.
They bow shyly as wet swans. They love each other.
There is no loneliness like theirs.
At home once more,
They begin munching the young tufts of spring in the
    darkness.
I would like to hold the slenderer one in my arms,
For she has walked over to me
And nuzzled my left hand.
She is black and white,
Her mane falls wild on her forehead,
And the light breeze moves me to caress her long ear
That is delicate as the skin over a girl's wrist.
Suddenly I realize
That if I stepped out of my body I would break
Into blossom.

Miners

THE police are dragging for the bodies
Of miners in the black waters
Of the suburbs.

Below, some few
Crawl, searching, until they clasp
The fingers of the sea.

Somewhere,
Beyond ripples and drowsing woodchucks,
A strong man, alone,
Beats on the door of a grave, crying
Oh let me in.

Many women mount long stairs
Into the shafts,
And emerge in the tottering palaces
Of abandoned cisterns.

In the middle of the night,
I can hear cars, moving on steel rails, colliding
Underground.

Lament

SOMEONE is dead.
Even the trees know it,
those poor old dancers who come on lewdly,
all pea-green scarfs and spine pole.
I think . . .
I think I could have stopped it,
if I'd been as firm as a nurse
or noticed the neck of the driver
as he cheated the crosstown lights;
or later in the evening,
if I'd held my napkin over my mouth.
I think I could . . .
if I'd been different, or wise, or calm,
I think I could have charmed the table,
the stained dish or the hand of the dealer.
But it's done.
It's all used up.
There's no doubt about the trees
spreading their thin feet into the dry grass.
A Canada goose rides up,
spread out like a gray suede shirt,
honking his nose into the March wind.
In the entryway a cat breathes calmly
into her watery blue fur.
The supper dishes are over and the sun
unaccustomed to anything else
goes all the way down.

Wanting to Die

SINCE you ask, most days I cannot remember.
I walk in my clothing, unmarked by that voyage.
Then the almost unnameable lust returns.

Even then I have nothing against life.
I know well the grass blades you mention,
the furniture you have placed under the sun.

But suicides have a special language.
Like carpenters they want to know *which tools*.
They never ask *why build*.

Twice I have so simply declared myself,
have possessed the enemy, eaten the enemy,
have taken on his craft, his magic.

In this way, heavy and thoughtful,
warmer than oil or water,
I have rested, drooling at the mouth-hole.

I did not think of my body at needle point.
Even the cornea and the leftover urine were gone.
Suicides have already betrayed the body.

Still-born, they don't always die,
but dazzled, they can't forget a drug so sweet
that even children would look on and smile.

To thrust all that life under your tongue! –
that, all by itself, becomes a passion.
Death's a sad bone; bruised, you'd say,

and yet she waits for me, year after year,
to so delicately undo an old wound,
to empty my breath from its bad prison.

Balanced there, suicides sometimes meet,
raging at the fruit, a pumped-up moon,
leaving the bread they mistook for a kiss,

leaving the page of the book carelessly open,
something unsaid, the phone off the hook
and the love, whatever it was, an infection.

3 February 1964

That Day

THIS is the desk I sit at
and this is the desk where I love you too much
and this is the typewriter that sits before me
where yesterday only your body sat before me
with its shoulders gathered in like a Greek chorus,
with its tongue like a king making up rules as he goes,
with its tongue quite openly like a cat lapping milk,
with its tongue – both of us coiled in its slippery life.
That was yesterday, that day.

That was the day of your tongue,
your tongue that came from your lips,
two openers, half animals, half birds
caught in the doorway of your heart.
That was the day I followed the king's rules,
passing by your red veins and your blue veins,
my hands down the backbone, down quick like a firepole,
hands between legs where you display your inner knowledge,
where diamond mines are buried and come forth to bury,
come forth more sudden than some reconstructed city.
It is complete within seconds, that monument.
The blood runs underground yet brings forth a tower.
A multitude should gather for such an edifice.
For a miracle one stands in line and throws confetti.
Surely The Press is here looking for headlines.
Surely someone should carry a banner on the sidewalk.

If a bridge is constructed doesn't the mayor cut a ribbon?
If a phenomenon arrives shouldn't the Magi come bearing
   gifts?
Yesterday was the day I bore gifts for your gift
and came from the valley to meet you on the pavement.
That was yesterday, that day.

That was the day of your face,
your face after love, close to the pillow, a lullaby.
Half asleep beside me letting the old fashioned rocker stop,
our breath became one, became a child-breath together,
while my fingers drew little o's on your shut eyes,
while my fingers drew little smiles on your mouth,
while I drew I LOVE YOU on your chest and its drummer
and whispered, 'Wake up!' and you mumbled in your sleep,
'Sh. We're driving to Cape Cod. We're heading for the
   Bourne
Bridge. We're circling around the Bourne Circle.' Bourne!
Then I knew you in your dream and prayed of our time
that I would be pierced and you would take root in me
and that I might bring forth your born, might bear
the you or the ghost of you in my little household.
Yesterday I did not want to be borrowed
but this is the typewriter that sits before me
and love is where yesterday is at.

The Long River

THE musk-ox smells
in his long head
my boat coming. When
I feel him there,
intent, heavy,

the oars make wings
in the white night,
and deep woods are close
on either side
where trees darken.

I rowed past towns
in their black sleep
to come here. I rowed
by northern grass
and cold mountains.

The musk-ox moves
when the boat stops,
in hard thickets. Now
the wood is dark
with old pleasures.

The Blue Wing

SHE was all around me
like a rainy day,
and though I walked bareheaded
I was not wet. I walked
on a bare path
singing light songs
about women.

A blue wing tilts at the edge of the sea.

The wreck of the small
airplane sleeps
drifted to the high tide line,
tangled in seaweed, green
glass from the sea.

The tiny skeleton inside
remembers the falter of engines, the
cry without
answer, the long dying
into
and out of the sea.

The Alligator Bride

THE clock of my days winds down.
The cat eats sparrows outside my window.
Once, she brought me a small rabbit
which we devoured together, under
the Empire Table
while the men shrieked
repossessing the gold umbrella.

Now the beard on my clock turns white.
My cat stares into dark corners
missing her gold umbrella.
She is in love
with the Alligator Bride.

Ah, the tiny fine white
teeth! The Bride, propped on her tail
in white lace
stares from the holes
of her eyes. Her stuck-open mouth
laughs at minister and people.

On bare new wood
fourteen tomatoes,
a dozen ears of corn,
six bottles of white wine,
a melon,
a cat,
broccoli
and the Alligator Bride.

The color of bubble gum,
the consistency of petroleum jelly,
wickedness oozes
from the palm of my left hand.
My cat licks it.
I watch the Alligator Bride.

Big houses like shabby boulders
hold themselves tight
in gelatin.
I am unable to daydream.
The sky is a gun aimed at me.
I pull the trigger.
The skull of my promises
leans in a black closet, gapes
with its good mouth
for a teat to suck.

A bird flies back and forth
in my house that is covered by gelatin
and the cat leaps at it
missing. Under the Empire Table
the Alligator Bride
lies in her bridal shroud.
My left hand
leaks on the Chinese carpet.

Gold

PALE gold of the walls, gold
of the centers of daisies, yellow roses
pressing from a clear bowl. All day
we lay on the huge bed, my hand
stroking the deep
gold of your thighs and your back.
We slept and woke
entering the golden room together,
lay down in it breathing
quickly, then
slowly again,
caressing and dozing, your hand sleepily
touching my hair now.

We made in those days
tiny identical rooms inside our bodies
which the men who uncover our graves
will find in a thousand years
shining and whole.

Reclining Figure

THEN the knee of the wave
turned to stone.

By the cliff of her flank
I anchored,

in the darkness of harbors
laid-by.

First Confession

BLOOD thudded in my ears. I scuffed,
   Steps stubborn, to the telltale booth
Beyond whose curtained portal coughed
   The robed repositor of truth.

The slat shot back. The universe
   Bowed down his cratered dome to hear
Enumerated my each curse,
   The sip snitched from my old man's beer,

My sloth pride envy lechery,
   The dime held back from Peter's Pence
With which I'd bribed my girl to pee
   That I might spy her instruments.

Hovering scale-pans when I'd done
   Settled their balance slow as silt
While in the restless dark I burned
   Bright as a brimstone in my guilt

Until as one feeds birds he doled
   Seven Our Fathers and a Hail
Which I to double-scrub my soul
   Intoned twice at the altar rail

Where Sunday in seraphic light
   I knelt, as full of grace as most,
And stuck my tongue out at the priest:
   A fresh roost for the Holy Ghost.

Nude Descending a Staircase

Toe upon toe, a snowing flesh,
A gold of lemon, root and rind,
She sifts in sunlight down the stairs
With nothing on. Nor on her mind.

We spy beneath the banister
A constant thresh of thigh on thigh —
Her lips imprint the swinging air
That parts to let her parts go by.

One-woman waterfall, she wears
Her slow descent like a long cape
And pausing, on the final stair
Collects her motions into shape.

Little Elegy
for a child who skipped rope

Here lies resting, out of breath,
Out of turns, Elizabeth
Whose quicksilver toes not quite
Cleared the whirring edge of night.

Earth whose circles round us skim
Till they catch the lightest limb,
Shelter now Elizabeth
And for her sake trip up death.

B Negative

M / 60 / 5 FT 4 / W PROT

You know it's April by the falling-off
In coughdrop boxes – fewer people cough –
  By daisies' first white eyeballs in the grass
And every dawn more underthings cast off.

Though plumtrees stretch recovered boughs to us
And doubledecked in green, the downtown bus,
  Love in one season – so your stab-pole tells –
Beds down, and buds, and is deciduous.

Now set down burlap bag. In pigeon talk
The wobbling pigeon flutes on the sidewalk,
  Struts on the breeze and clicks leisurely wings
As if the corn he ate grew on a stalk.

So plump he topples where he tries to stand,
He pecks my shoelaces, come to demand
  Another sack, another fifteen cents,
And yet – who else will eat out of my hand?

It used to be that when I laid my head
And body with it down by you in bed
  You did not turn from me nor fall to sleep
But turn to fall between my arms instead

And now I lay bifocals down. My feet
Forget the twist that brought me to your street.
  I can't make out your face for steamed-up glass
Nor quite call back your outline on the sheet.

I know how, bent to a movie magazine,
The hobo's head lights up, and from its screen
  Imagined bosoms in slow motion bloom
And no director interrupts the scene.

I used to purchase in the Automat
A cup of soup and fan it with my hat
   Until a stern voice from the changebooth crashed
Like nickels: *Gentlemen do not do that.*

Spring has no household, no abiding heat,
Pokes forth no bud from branches of concrete,
   Nothing to touch you, nothing you can touch —
The snow, at least, keeps track of people's feet.

The springer spaniel and the buoyant hare
Seem half at home reclining in mid-air —
   But, Lord, the times I've leaped the way they do
And looked round for a foothold — in despair.

The subway a little cheaper than a room,
I browse the *News* — or so the guards assume —
   And there half-waking, tucked in funny-sheets,
I hurtle in my mileaminute womb.

Down streets that wake up earlier than wheels
The routed spirit flees on dusty heels
   And in the soft fire of a muscatel
Sits up, puts forth its fingertips, and feels —

Down streets so deep the sun can't vault their walls,
Where one-night wives make periodic calls,
   Where cat steals stone where rat makes off with child
And lyre and lute lie down under three balls,

Down blocks in sequence, fact by separate fact,
The human integers add and subtract
   Till in a cubic room in some hotel
You wake one day to find yourself abstract

And turn a knob and hear a voice: *Insist
On Jiffy Blades, they're tender to the wrist* —
   Then static, then a squawk as if your hand
Had shut a human windpipe with a twist.

I know how, lurking under trees by dark,
Poor loony stranglers out to make their mark
   Reach forth shy hands to touch some woman's hair —
I pick up after them in Central Park.

In a Prominent Bar in Secaucus One Day

*(To the tune of 'The Old Orange Flute' or the tune of 'Sweet
Betsy from Pike')*

In a prominent bar in Secaucus one day
Rose a lady in skunk with a topheavy sway,
Raised a knobby red finger — all turned from their beer —
While with eyes bright as snowcrust she sang high and clear:

'Now who of you'd think from an eyeload of me
That I once was a lady as proud as could be?
Oh I'd never sit down by a tumbledown drunk
If it wasn't, my dears, for the high cost of junk.

'All the gents used to swear that the white of my calf
Beat the down of the swan by a length and a half.
In the kerchief of linen I caught to my nose
Ah, there never fell snot, but a little gold rose.

'I had seven gold teeth and a toothpick of gold,
My Virginia cheroot was a leaf of it rolled
And I'd light it each time with a thousand in cash —
Why the bums used to fight if I flicked them an ash.

'Once the toast of the Biltmore, the belle of the Taft,
I would drink bottle beer at the Drake, never draught,
And dine at the Astor on Salisbury steak
With a clean tablecloth for each bite I did take.

'In a car like the Roxy I'd roll to the track,
A steel-guitar trio, a bar in the back,
And the wheels made no noise, they turned over so fast,
Still it took you ten minutes to see me go past.

'When the horses bowed down to me that I might choose,
I bet on them all, for I hated to lose.
Now I'm saddled each night for my butter and eggs
And the broken threads race down the backs of my legs.

'Let you hold in mind, girls, that your beauty must pass
Like a lovely white clover that rusts with its grass.
Keep your bottoms off barstools and marry you young
Or be left – an old barrel with many a bung.

'For when time takes you out for a spin in his car
You'll be hard-pressed to stop him from going too far
And be left by the roadside, for all your good deeds,
Two toadstools for tits and a face full of weeds.'

All the house raised a cheer, but the man at the bar
Made a phonecall and up pulled a red patrol car
And she blew us a kiss as they copped her away
From that prominent bar in Secaucus, N. J.

The Insusceptibles

THEN the long sunlight lying on the sea
Fell, folded gold on gold; and slowly we
Took up our decks of cards, our parasols,
The picnic hamper and the sandblown shawls
And climbed the dunes in silence. There were two
Who lagged behind as lovers sometimes do,
And took a different road. For us the night
Was final, and by artificial light
We came indoors to sleep. No envy there
Of those who might be watching anywhere
The lustres of the summer dark, to trace
Some vagrant splinter blazing out of space.
No thought of them, save in a lower room
To leave a light for them when they should come.

Readings of History

'He delighted in relating the fact that he had been born near Girgenti
in a place called Chaos during a raging cholera epidemic'
DOMENICO VITTORINI,
The Drama of Luigi Pirandello

I

The Evil Eye

LAST night we sat with the stereopticon,
laughing at genre view of 1906,
till suddenly, gazing straight into
that fringed and tasselled parlour, where the vestal
spurns an unlikely suitor

with hairy-crested plants to right and left,
my heart sank. It was terrible.
I smelled the mildew in those swags of plush,
dust on the eyepiece bloomed to freaks of mould.
I knew beyond all doubt how dead that couple was.

Today, a fresh clean morning.
Your camera stabs me unawares,
right in my mortal part.
A womb of celluloid already
contains my dotage and my total absence.

II

The Confrontation

Luigi Pirandello
looked like an old historian
(oval head, tufted white beard,
not least the hunger
for reconciliation in his eye).
For fourteen years, facing
his criminal reflection
in his wife's Grand Guignol mind,
he built over and over
that hall of mirrors
in which to be appears
to be perceived.

The present holds you like a raving wife,
clever as the mad are clever,
digging up your secret truths
from her disabled genius.
She knows what you hope
and dare not hope:
remembers
what you're sick of forgetting.

What are you now
but what you know together, you and she?
She will not let you think.
It is important to get away
to make connexions. Everything
happens very fast in the minds
of the insane. Even you
aren't up to that, yet.
Go out, walk,
think of selves long past.

III

Memorabilia

I recall
Civil War letters of a great-grand-uncle,
fifteen at Chancellorsville,
                        no raconteur,
no speller, either; nor, to put it squarely,
much of a mind;
                        the most we gather
is that he did write home:
                        I am well,
how are my sisters, hope you are the same.
Did Spartan battle-echoes rack his head?
Dying, he turned into his father's memory.

History's queerly strong perfumes
rise from the crook of this day's elbow:
Seduction fantasies of the public mind,
or Dilthey's dream from which he roused to see
the cosmos glaring through his windowpane?
Prisoners of what we think occurred,
or dreamers dreaming toward a final word?

What, in fact, happened in these woods
on some obliterated afternoon?

IV

Consanguinity

Can history show us nothing
but pieces of ourselves, detached,
set to a kind of poetry,
a kind of music, even?
Seated today on Grandmamma's
plush sofa with the grapes
bursting so ripely from the curved mahogany,
we read the great Victorians
weeping, almost, as if
some family breach were healed.
Those angry giantesses and giants,
lately our kith and kin!
We stare into their faces, hear
at last what they were saying
(or some version not bruited
by filial irritation).

The cat-tails wither in the reading-room.
Tobacco-coloured dust
drifts on the newest magazines.
I skulk here leafing ancient copies
of LIFE from World War II.
We look so poor and honest there:
girls with long hair badly combed
and unbecoming dresses –
where are you now?
                  You sail
to shop in Europe, ignorantly saved
for you, an age ago.
Your nylon luggage matches
                          eyelids
expertly azured.
I, too, have lived in history.

V

The Mirror

Is it in hopes
to find or lose myself
that I
fill up my table now
with Michelet and Motley?
to 'know how it was'
or to forget how it is —
what else?
Split at the root, neither Gentile nor Jew,
Yankee nor Rebel, born
in the face of two ancient cults,
I'm a good reader of histories.
And you,
Morris Cohen, dear to me as a brother,
when you sit at night
tracing your way through your volumes
of Josephus, or any
of the old Judaic chronicles,
do you find yourself there, a simpler
more eloquent Jew?
                    or do you read
to shut out the tick-tock of self,
the questions and their routine answers?

VI

The Covenant

The present breaks our hearts. We lie and freeze,
our fingers icy as a bunch of keys.
Nothing will thaw these bones except
memory like an ancient blanket wrapped
about us when we sleep at home again,
smelling of picnics, closets, sicknesses,

old nightmare,
                    and insomnia's spreading stain.
Or say I sit with what I halfway know
as with a dying man who heaves the true
version at last, now that it hardly matters,
or gropes a hand to where the letters
sewn in the mattress can be plucked and read.
Here's water.   Sleep.   No more is asked of you.
I take your life into my living head.

Phi Beta Kappa poem, 1960, College of William and Mary

Home on the Range, February 1962

FLUTES, and the harp on the plain
Is a distance, of pain, and waving reeds
The scale of far off trees, notes not of course
Upon a real harp but chords in the thick clouds
And the wind reaching its arms toward west yellowstone
Moving to the east, the grass was high once, and before
White wagons moved
                    the hawk, proctor of the hills still is

Oh god did the chunky westerner think to remake this in his
    own image
Oh god did the pioneer society sanctify the responsible
    citizen
To do that
           face like a plot of ground
Was it iron locomotives and shovels were hand tools
And barbed wire motives for each man's
Fenced off little promised land

                or the mind of bent

Or of carson, oh earp
These sherpas of responsible destruction
Posses led by a promising girl wielding a baton upon the
    street
A Sacagawea wearing a baseball cap, eating a Clark bar.
And flutes and the harp are on the plain to
Bring the last leading edge of stillness
Brought no water, brought dead roots
Like an allotment of tool handles to their premises – and they
    cry
In pain over daily income – a hundred years of planned greed

Loving the welfare state of new barns and bean drills
Hot passion for the freedom of the dentist!
Their plots were america's first subdivisions called home-
steads

Lean american – gothic quarter sections gaunt look
Managing to send their empty headed son who is a ninny
To nebraska to do it, all over again, to the ground, a prairie
Dog hole,
And always they smirk at starvation
And consider it dirty . . . a joke their daughters learn
From their new husbands.

On the Debt My Mother Owed to Sears Roebuck

SUMMER was dry, dry the garden
our beating hearts, on that farm, dry
with the rows of corn the grasshoppers
came happily to strip, in hordes, the first
thing I knew about locust was they came
dry under the foot like the breaking of
a mechanical bare heart which collapses
from an unkind an incessant word whispered
in the house of the major farmer
and the catalogue company,
from no fault of anyone
my father coming home tired
and grinning down the road, turning in
is the tank full? thinking of the horse
and my lazy arms thinking of the water
so far below the well platform.

On the debt my mother owed to sears roebuck
we brooded, she in the house, a little heavy
from too much corn meal, she
a little melancholy from the dust of the fields
in her eye, the only title she ever had to lands –

and man's ways winged their way to her through the mail
saying so much per month
so many months, this is yours, take it
take it, take it, take it
and in the corncrib, like her lives in that house
the mouse nibbled away at the cob's yellow grain
until six o'clock when her sorrows grew less
and my father came home

On the debt my mother owed to sears roebuck?
I have nothing to say, it gave me clothes to
wear to school,
and my mother brooded

   in the rooms of the house, the kitchen, waiting
for the men she knew, her husband, her son
from work, from school, from the air of locusts
and dust masking the hedges of fields she knew
in her eye as a vague land where she lived,
boundaries, whose tractors chugged pulling harrows
pulling discs, pulling great yields from the earth
pulse for the armies in two hemispheres, 1943
and she was part of that *stay at home army* to keep
things going, owing that debt.

A Song

THERE is a blue sky
over the flower, there is
a green sea beneath
yet there is no bliss
along my way now . . .

In the casual flight of this day
there is a yellow flower edged
in blue
there is a sky filled with snow

and along my way there few bright calls
of spring, there is hardly a chance
there are ahead no tricks
to turn a season, all friends
are sober.

I have a dark blue sky
inside my head, ah,
there is a flower here
and there, and yes, believe
I'll miss this time, sometime,
these old cold mountains
these cold blue hills
sometime.

Mourning Letter, March 29 1963

No hesitation
                    would stay me
from weeping this morning
for the miners of Hazard Kentucky.
                    The mine owners'
extortionary skulls
whose eyes are diamonds don't float
down the rivers, as they should,
of the flood

                    The miners, cold
starved, driven from work, in
their homes float though and float
on the ribbed ships of their frail
bodies.

                    Oh, go letter,
keep my own misery close to theirs
associate me with no other honor.

All through the Rains

THAT mare stood in the field –
A big pine-tree and a shed,
But she stayed in the open
Ass to the wind, splash wet.
I tried to catch her April
For a bareback ride,
She kicked and bolted
Later grazing fresh shoots
In the shade of the down
Eucalyptus on the hill.

Piute Creek

ONE granite ridge
A tree, would be enough
Or even a rock, a small creek,
A bark-shred in a pool.
Hill beyond hill, folded and twisted
Tough trees crammed
In thin stone fractures
A huge moon on it all, is too much.
The mind wanders. A million
Summers, night air still and the rocks
Warm. Sky over endless mountains.
All the junk that goes with being human
Drops away, hard rock wavers
Even the heavy present seems to fail
This bubble of a heart.

Words and books
Like a small creek off a high ledge
Gone in the dry air.
A clear, attentive mind
Has no meaning but that
Which sees is truly seen.
No one loves rock, yet we are here.
Night chills. A flick
In the moonlight
Slips into Juniper shadow:
Back there unseen
Cold proud eyes
Of Cougar or Coyote
Watch me rise and go.

Above Pate Valley

WE finished clearing the last
Section of trail by noon,
High on the ridge-side
Two thousand feet above the creek –
Reached the pass, went on
Beyond the white pine groves,
Granite shoulders, to a small
Green meadow watered by the snow,
Edged with Aspen – sun
Straight high and blazing
But the air was cool.
Ate a cold fried trout in the
Trembling shadows. I spied
A glitter, and found a flake
Black volcanic glass – obsidian –
By a flower. Hands and knees

Pushing the Bear grass, thousands
Of arrowhead leavings over a
Hundred yards. Not one good
Head, just razor flakes
On a hill snowed all but summer,
A land of fat summer deer,
They came to camp. On their
Own trails. I followed my own
Trail here. Picked up the cold-drill,
Pick, singlejack, and sack
Of dynamite.
Ten thousand years.

Milton by Firelight
(Piute Creek, August 1955)

'O HELL, what do mine eyes
        with grief behold?'
Working with an old
Singlejack miner, who can sense
The vein and cleavage
In the very guts of rock, can
Blast granite, build
Switchbacks that last for years
Under the beat of snow, thaw, mule-hooves.
What use, Milton, a silly story
Of our lost general parents,
        eaters of fruit?

The Indian, the chainsaw boy,
And a string of six mules
Came riding down to camp
Hungry for tomatoes and green apples.

Sleeping in saddle-blankets
Under a bright night-sky
Han River slantwise by morning.
Jays squall
Coffee boils

In ten thousand years the Sierras
Will be dry and dead, home of the scorpion.
Ice-scratched slabs and bent trees.
No paradise, no fall,
Only the weathering land
The wheeling sky,
Man, with his Satan
Scouring the chaos of the mind.
Oh Hell!

Fire down
Too dark to read, miles from a road
The bell-mare clangs in the meadow
That packed dirt for a fill-in
Scrambling through loose rocks
On an old trail
All of a summer's day.

Hay for the Horses

HE had driven half the night
From far down San Joaquin
Through Mariposa, up the
Dangerous mountain roads,
And pulled in at eight a.m.
With his big truckload of hay
            behind the barn.

With winch and ropes and hooks
We stacked the bales up clean
To splintery redwood rafters
High in the dark, flecks of alfalfa
Whirling through shingle-cracks of light,
Itch of haydust in the
          sweaty shirt and shoes.
At lunchtime under Black oak
Out in the hot corral,
– The old mare nosing lunchpails,
  Grasshoppers crackling in the weeds –
'I'm sixty-eight,' he said,
'I first bucked hay when I was seventeen.
I thought, that day I started,
I sure would hate to do this all my life.
And dammit, that's just what
I've gone and done.'

Lady Lazarus

I HAVE done it again.
One year in every ten
I manage it —

A sort of walking miracle, my skin
Bright as a Nazi lampshade,
My right foot

A paperweight,
My face a featureless, fine
Jew linen.

Peel off the napkin
O my enemy.
Do I terrify? —

The nose, the eye pits, the full set of teeth?
The sour breath
Will vanish in a day.

Soon, soon the flesh
The grave cave ate will be
At home on me

And I a smiling woman.
I am only thirty.
And like the cat I have nine times to die.

This is Number Three.
What a trash
To annihilate each decade.

What a million filaments.
The peanut-crunching crowd
Shoves in to see

Them unwrap me hand and foot –
The big strip tease.
Gentlemen, ladies

These are my hands
My knees.
I may be skin and bone,

Nevertheless, I am the same, identical woman.
The first time it happened I was ten.
It was an accident.

The second time I meant
To last it out and not come back at all.
I rocked shut

As a seashell.
They had to call and call
And pick the worms off me like sticky pearls.

Dying
Is an art, like everything else.
I do it exceptionally well.

I do it so it feels like hell.
I do it so it feels real.
I guess you could say I've a call.

It's easy enough to do it in a cell.
It's easy enough to do it and stay put.
It's the theatrical

Comeback in broad day
To the same place, the same face, the same brute
Amused shout:

'A miracle!'
That knocks me out.
There is a charge

For the eyeing of my scars, there is a charge
For the hearing of my heart –
It really goes.

And there is a charge, a very large charge
For a word or a touch
Or a bit of blood

Or a piece of my hair or my clothes.
So, so, Herr Doktor.
So, Herr Enemy.

I am your opus,
I am your valuable,
The pure gold baby

That melts to a shriek.
I turn and burn.
Do not think I underestimate your great concern.

Ash, ash –
You poke and stir.
Flesh, bone, there is nothing there –

A cake of soap,
A wedding ring,
A gold filling.

Herr God, Herr Lucifer
Beware
Beware.

Out of the ash
I rise with my red hair
And I eat men like air.

Death & Co.

Two, of course there are two.
It seems perfectly natural now –
The one who never looks up, whose eyes are lidded
And balled, like Blake's,
Who exhibits

The birthmarks that are his trademark –
The scald scar of water,
The nude
Verdigris of the condor.
I am red meat. His beak

Claps sidewise: I am not his yet.
He tells me how badly I photograph.
He tells me how sweet
The babies look in their hospital
Icebox, a simple

Frill at the neck,
Then the flutings of their Ionian
Death-gowns,
Then two little feet.
He does not smile or smoke.

The other does that,
His hair long and plausive.
Bastard
Masturbating a glitter,
He wants to be loved.

I do not stir.
The frost makes a flower,
The dew makes a star,
The dead bell,
The dead bell.

Somebody's done for.

Words

Axes
After whose stroke the wood rings,
And the echoes!
Echoes travelling
Off from the centre like horses.

The sap
Wells like tears, like the
Water striving
To re-establish its mirror
Over the rock

That drops and turns,
A white skull,
Eaten by weedy greens.
Years later I
Encounter them on the road –

Words dry and riderless,
The indefatigable hoof-taps.
While
From the bottom of the pool, fixed stars
Govern a life.

Hard Rock Returns to Prison from the Hospital for the Criminal Insane

HARD Rock was 'known not to take no shit
From nobody,' and he had the scars to prove it:
Split purple lips, lumped ears, welts above
His yellow eyes, and one long scar that cut
Across his temple and plowed through a thick
Canopy of kinky hair.

The WORD was that Hard Rock wasn't a mean nigger
Anymore, that the doctors had bored a hole in his head,
Cut out part of his brain, and shot electricity
Through the rest. When they brought Hard Rock back,
Handcuffed and chained, he was turned loose,
Like a freshly gelded stallion, to try his new status.
And we all waited and watched, like indians at a corral,
To see if the WORD was true.

As we waited we wrapped ourselves in the cloak
Of his exploits: 'Man, the last time, it took eight
Screws to put him in the Hole.' 'Yeah, remember when he
Smacked the captain with his dinner tray?' 'He set
The record for time in the Hole – 67 straight days!'
'Ol Hard Rock! man, that's one crazy nigger.'
And then the jewel of a myth that Hard Rock had once bit
A screw on the thumb and poisoned him with syphilitic spit.

The testing came, to see if Hard Rock was really tame.
A hillbilly called him a black son of a bitch
And didn't lose his teeth, a screw who knew Hard Rock
From before shook him down and barked in his face.
And Hard Rock did *nothing*. Just grinned and looked silly,
His eyes empty like knot holes in a fence.

And even after we discovered that it took Hard Rock
Exactly 3 minutes to tell you his first name,
We told ourselves that he had just wised up,
Was being cool; but we could not fool ourselves for long,
And we turned away, our eyes on the ground. Crushed.
He had been our Destroyer, the doer of things
We dreamed of doing but could not bring ourselves to do,
The fears of years, like a biting whip,
Had cut grooves too deeply across our backs.

He Sees Through Stone

HE sees through stone
he has the secret
eyes this old black one
who under prison skies
sits pressed by the sun
against the western wall
his pipe between purple gums

the years fall
like overripe plums
bursting red flesh
on the dark earth

his time is not my time
but I have known him
in a time gone

he led me trembling cold
into the dark forest
taught me the secret rites
to take a woman
to be true to my brothers
to make my spear drink
the blood
of my enemies

now black cats circle him
flash white teeth
snarl at the air
mashing green grass beneath
shining muscles
ears peeling his words
he smiles
he knows
the hunt the enemy
he has the secret eyes
he sees through stone

The Idea of Ancestry

I

TAPED to the wall of my cell are 47 pictures: 47 black
faces: my father, mother, grandmothers (1 dead), grand
fathers (both dead), brothers, sisters, uncles, aunts,
cousins (1st & 2nd), nieces, and nephews. They stare
across the space at me sprawling on my bunk. I know
their dark eyes, they know mine. I know their style,
they know mine. I am all of them, they are all of me;
they are farmers, I am a thief, I am me, they are thee.

I have at one time or another been in love with my mother,
1 grandmother, 2 sisters, 2 aunts (1 went to the asylum),
and 5 cousins. I am now in love with a 7 yr old niece
(she sends me letters written in large block print, and
her picture is the only one that smiles at me).

I have the same name as 1 grandfather, 3 cousins, 3 nephews,
and 1 uncle. The uncle disappeared when he was 15, just took
off and caught a freight (they say). He's discussed each year
when the family has a reunion, he causes uneasiness in
the clan, he is an empty space. My father's mother, who is 93

and who keeps the Family Bible with everybody's birth dates (and death dates) in it, always mentions him. There is no place in her Bible for 'whereabouts unknown'.

II

Each Fall the graves of my grandfathers call me, the brown hills and red gullies of mississippi send out their electric messages, galvanizing my genes. Last yr/like a salmon quitting
the cold ocean – leaping and bucking up his birthstream/I hitchhiked my way from L.A. with 16 caps in my pocket and a monkey on my back. and I almost kicked it with the kinfolks.
I walked barefooted in my grandmother's backyard/I smelled the old
land and the woods/I sipped cornwhiskey from fruit jars with the men/
I flirted with the women/I had a ball till the caps ran out and my habit came down. That night I looked at my grand-mother
and split/my guts were screaming for junk/but I was almost contented/I had almost caught up with me.
(The next day in Memphis I cracked a croaker's crib for a fix.)

This yr there is a gray stone wall damming my stream, and when
the falling leaves stir my genes, I pace my cell or flop on my bunk
and stare at 47 black faces across the space. I am all of them, they are all of me, I am me, they are thee, and I have no sons to float in the space between.

As You Leave Me

SHINY record albums scattered over
the livingroom floor, reflecting light
from the lamp, sharp reflections that hurt
my eyes as I watch you, squatting among the platters,
the beer foam making mustaches on your lips.

And, too,
the shadows on your cheeks from your long lashes
fascinate me – almost as much as the dimples:
in your cheeks, your arms and your legs:
dimples . . . dimples . . . dimples . . .

You
hum along with Mathis – how you love Mathis!
with his burnished hair and quicksilver voice that dances
among the stars and whirls through canyons
like windblown snow. sometimes I think that Mathis
could take you from me if you could be complete
without me. I glance at my watch. it is now time.

You rise,
silently, and to the bedroom and the paint:
on the lips red, on the eyes black,
and I lean in the doorway and smoke, and see you
grow old before my eyes, and smoke. why do you
chatter while you dress, and smile when you grab
your large leather purse? don't you know that when you
leave me I walk to the window and watch you? and light
a reefer as I watch you? and I die as I watch you
disappear in the dark streets
to whistle and to smile at the johns.

The European Shoe

THE European Shoe is constructed of grass and reed, bound up and wound around so that it may slip easily over the wearers' head.

In case you are an aircraft pilot, you must take care that the European Shoe does not creep off your foot, and begin to make its way carefully along the fuselage.

The European Shoe pressed against the fugitive's nose, preventing it from imminent departure.

The European Shoe spends summers in delightful ways. A lady feels its subtle and unexpected pressure the length of her decolletage. (It winters in pain.)

That time I lent you my European Shoe you departed with a look of grandeur, and in total disrepair.

The European Shoe knocks on the door of the carefree farmerette. 'The harvest has been gathered in, ha, ha,' it says, moving shyly forth along the edge of the couch.

I pointed to the European Shoe. I ate the European Shoe. I married the European Shoe.

Tears fall from the eye of the European Shoe as it waves goodbye to us from the back balcony of the speeding train.

It helps an old lady, extremely crippled and arthritic, move an enormous cornerstone. It invents a watch, which, when wound up tightly, flies completely to pieces.

It was a simple and dignified ceremony, distinguished for its gales of uncontrollable laughter, in which I married the European Shoe.

If it rains, the European Shoe becomes very heavy. I failed to cross the river, where thousands of European shoes lay capsized.

And so we lived alone, we two, the envy of our neighborhoods, the delight of our lively hordes of children.

I saw a flightful of graceful swallows heading to distant, half-forgotten islands over the distant seas; and in the midst of that annually questing company, I saw the European Shoe.

It never harmed anyone, and yet it never helped anyone.

Gaily it sets out into the depths of my profoundest closet, to do battle with the dusts of summer.

The Eye

THE narcissist's eye is blue, fringed with white and covered with tempting salad leaves.

The purse-stealer's eye is yellow.

The eye of the non-combatant is white. In the center is a target rendered in green and black.

The voluptuary's eye comes to a point. It is like a silo, the echo of a halo.

The gravedigger's eye is hollow. It is surrounded by a thoroughly contemporary serenity.

The dynamite salesman's eye is like a pool, in which he who leans to drink may be lost. Drifting forever, like a cloud.

The maiden's eye is tucked under.

The billiard-player's eye comes to a point. It is like a mild wine. Each billiard-player suffers from imperfect nostalgia.

The ghost's eye is green.

The poet's eye is like a candy.

The battleship captain's eye is like the light that falls in a glen,
    when the doe has done with drinking.

The eye of the realist is inflatable.

Divine Love

A LIP which had once been stolid, now moving
Gradually around the side of the head
Eye-like
The eye twisted on the end of somebody's finger and spinning
Around the sun, its ear,
And the brain aloft over the lake of the face –
Near the cataract of the body –
Like a cumulus cloud enlarged before a rainstorm:

A sound
That grows gradually in the East
Driving everything before it: cattle and rainbows and lovers
Swept on
To the table of the body at which five men and two women
    are casually sitting down to eat

Some Feelings

THE feelings go up into the air
Rising in lines that are straight until they bump
Into something
A building
With its roof overhanging, a judge
Who is looking out of the window attempting to see that
    nurse
Changing uniforms which are transparent anyway in a
    neighboring indoor hospital yard
Music (the feelings sift through little drifting notes from a
    radio);

Then they continue
Rising so swiftly and so purely they seem to supersede all
   objects

Only somebody
At the level of the ground may see
That each feeling is connected by a thread to a forehead, an
   arm, or a leg
And that individuals
At the heights of their tragic moments
Resemble porcupines or pincushions.

Thoughts

EXCUSE me, isn't that you I see concealed underneath there
Inside the shield, or conning tower, of your head,
Your eyes looking out of the perforations in your flesh?
How can you think you can see from out of liquid, anyway?
   Are rain puddles watching me even now,
And can ducts which punctuate the underground of a field
Examine it at will for buried treasure? Is the rain outside your
   window a voyeur, then? Deep down under all that, though,
Underneath the liquids and the various unobservant stuffs
There is a spirit, shifting around from foot to foot.

Poem

the tiny new emotions
no doubt left
everything clear in a deceiving light
and the tresses of a beloved
forming a collar that presses
to quell the passion of the blood
the autumn strict of the eye

the plumage of the intellect lies steeped
in feces and blood
o beech, unbind your leaf, for deep
in its yellow
the honeyed lime lies sleeping
and lead shade
seals up the eyelids of its sheep
and the reprieve tolls gluelike
no awakening
now the rich cherry

now all the spring and autumn trees

Going to School in France or America

DRUGS are a tuition,
and tuition is teaching,
but in French *tuer* is to kill,
and so in France drugs are killing.

What does it mean to 'make a killing'?
It means to make money,
and money is a means
to certain kinds of killing,

as for instance dropping millions of pennies
on someone from a helicopter.
Money can also be used to buy drugs, helicopters,
or to pay for your tuition,

but money, drugs, and killing
are not the sort of pursuits
a person should pursue with his tuition
if he is a student in France or America.

Doors

A LOVE that is not pardoned
But burns the hand that touches
The wind
Tears her form out of the corner
Something presses me her voice
Across the sea a light is lifted
A woman walks to the edge
Of the mud in the street clinging to her packages

In the car of the sea these rusted shapes
Take up the night with a music like stone
The door will not close
Smoke   The cotton
Stuffing of the room
Flatness under my feet walking around the room
A weight on my tongue
The stone fenders are close to the water
At any step you might fall
Things are going badly now
Nothing swims up through
The metal that holds the muddy flowers

There is dirt in every space and a cold wind
Comes off the sea

Pleats of the bedclothes make a hole in the light
A dirty shadow on the door above your head
And the wall bends up losing you
As far apart as it can go
Breaking into pieces like a bird
We go at different speeds
Side by side while you sleep

It is grey ahead where I am going

It is too hot
All rooms beat constantly
Something is the matter with the doors but no one stops
We rush through the joys that were there
The same weight of confusion leads me
To pick up everything I find
I turn this over in my hand and find you
Your hands are behind your head
Forming a grave on the pillows
Reality only listens when your words are true
How much longer can the door be found
By picking strings
To a chamber where a vestment
Never speaks until the door to the other side
Upward through the mud to the spoons
Has been closed
A chorus of swine lets loose

In a grey corner the rats continue to sing
Most of this is useless
An insane need for genuflecting
The night flaps
I stand at the edge of you
Is there a switch to be turned
To end this bluff against music
Which outshines the diamond in the slush
All of us wanted to have

Are there green parks where bicycles still glide
We sat on the hills quarreling
As you undress the perfection
Of hair marking each part of you
That seeps down through
This maze of pictures
I carry like sections of cloth d'or
In ancient painting there is a duel in which
There are
Wings beating in something like hay
Beyond which the mystery is encountered again
She replaces the packages under her arms
And walks through the door

Eyeglasses

OF this house I know the backwindow
lodges six housesparrows in the bricks

Under the sill, and they are the birds
scour these roofs all winter for warmth

Or whatever. Two are arguing now
for a few inches of position on a cornice.

How the mind moves out and lights on things
when the *I* is only a glass for seeing:

I stand at the window

Setting down each bird, roof, chimney
as the boundaries of the neighborhood they make.

I have on an old blue jersey.
Every two hours I wipe off my glasses.

Poem

LIKE musical instruments
Abandoned in a field
The parts of your feelings

Are starting to know a quiet
The pure conversion of your
Life into art seems destined

Never to occur
You don't mind
You feel spiritual and alert

As the air must feel
Turning into sky aloft and blue
You feel like

You'll never feel like touching anything or anyone
Again
And then you do

After the Broken Arm

FROM point A a wind is blowing to point B
Which is here, where the pebble is only a mountain.
If truly heaven and earth are out there
Why is that man waving his arms around,
Gesturing to the word 'lightning' written on the clouds
That surround and disguise his feet?

If you say the right word in New York City
Nothing will happen in New York City;
But out in the fabulous dry horror of the west
A beautiful girl named Sibyl will burst
In by the open window breathless
And settle for an imaginary glass of something.
But now her name is no longer Sibyl – it's Herman,
Yearning for point B.

Dispatch this note to our hero at once.

The Sandwich Man

THE funny thing is that he's reading a paper
As if with his throat
With the bottom half folded neatly under his chin
Which is, incidentally, clean-shaven
As he strolls absently toward us, toting a sewing machine
On the front
With delicate little gold lines curling and swaying below a
    white spool in the afternoon

A dog barks – well, arf! you pull the cord attached to the
    monastery
Bell that rings utterly somewhere else
Perhaps the cord is ringing
And you are a Russian
In some hideously small town
Or worst of all
You're listening to the story behind the bell
A history whose rugged but removed features
Resemble those of the sandwich man
Not the one that wandered off into the swamp
Cuffs filled with wind
And was never seen again
But this new one who overestimates his duty by teaching
School in a place that has as students
At best only a bunch of heavily panting dogs
Seated in rows of wooden and iron desks linked
Like slaves on a dismal galley, the Ship of Genius
Sailing for some points known and a few unknown
Caring little about either, huffing away
Toward the horizon destroyed by other students...
    estudianti

One of these others, the head, is in fact the Infanta,
In reality only a very intelligent little girl
But beyond the immense corrugated brook we know of as
    this earth
Covered with raving, a constellation in the shape of a bullet –
She always did love the sound of a ricochet – and I too
Can hear it often, at night, before I go to sleep
In my nose
        In Spain, ah
In Spain there are the prune fields and the dark
Beauty of a prune now lowers a shade
Past the sewing machine, over which blow long, regular
    waves of dust particles

In one of which a medium-sized boy in white sandals is
   peddling up to
Offer you a worried rose

Rose . . . but I know nothing of this rose
Although I will draw it for you in words if you wish
Clockwise beginning at noon on the outer rim
On the first petal is a cave and the second a squiggle
The third a proper noun or else a common noun beginning a
   sentence
Or even perhaps a noun capitalized for no reason at all, for
   God's sake!

Japan!   Penitentiary!

That's what we want!
To move and dance
With strangers, people we don't know
With lines and circles going through us
Who are the landscape

Whose clouds are really toots from the nearby factory
I love so much, the steam factory, making steam
For people to fall down on and permit their bodies to vibrate
Occasionally a straw hat is flung through the factory window
And sails spinning into the water

It is night

A dog barks outside the window
Either that or the window's silent in the dog
— You'll say I'm playing the overture
And finale off against each other, after all
There's no other way to locate the middle,
Which is more elusive than it might seem:
The fifty yard line does escape
The gridiron, extending itself through
Both grandstands, through you and me, plus

A parking lot now indistinguishable from the fog, backyards,
    dreams, washing . . .
And the large peanut that has come to stand for something
    beautiful and intelligent
In short, civilization.

Not so! says a man in striped pants wheeled in out of the
    moonlight
You think this only because you associate this object with
    yourselves
. . . which is okay by me . . .
He was wheeled out and chucked over the balcony
Into the magnolia bushes.

At dawn, I find one other example, though nearly driven
    away
By the dust on it:
You are, say, six feet tall
Or six feet long
In the first instance you are an active human being other than
    a baby
In the second you are either a very large baby or
A corpse or perhaps a bed-ridden invalid or
Two yardsticks placed end to end. What your six feet
Would be were you tilted at 45° angle
I do not know
Doubtless a census taker's nightmare, in which bent
Horrible monsters jump out and bite him

The next step is to know that this fuzzy angle is true in your
    heart
But not to know what happens to it
When it leaves there, flowers gushing out . . .
It appears in Amsterdam always
City of extension cords
And ladies with boxes of rubber bands and

A truly horrible music washing the streets rushing below the
   pigeons
That now seem to be following him as sure as iron
Follows a crook

I don't think I can stand it! the birds
Are swooping down in and out of a large design yes!
A police car is pulling itself together
In the skies, its headlights on now
Bearing down on the sandwich man, still reading,
Whose next step puts him behind
Us as we turn ourselves around to see his other board
And the horrible license plate on it

INDEXES

INDEX OF POETS

INDEX OF TITLES

INDEX OF FIRST LINES

FOR THE BEST IN PAPERBACKS, LOOK FOR THE 🐧

In every corner of the world, on every subject under the sun, Penguin represents quality and variety – the very best in publishing today.

For complete information about books available from Penguin – including Pelicans, Puffins, Peregrines and Penguin Classics – and how to order them, write to us at the appropriate address below. Please note that for copyright reasons the selection of books varies from country to country.

FOR THE BEST IN PAPERBACKS, LOOK FOR THE 🐧

PENGUIN BOOKS OF POETRY

American Verse
Ballads
British Poetry Since 1945
Caribbean Verse
A Choice of Comic and Curious Verse
Contemporary American Poetry
Contemporary British Poetry
Eighteenth-Century Verse
Elizabethan Verse
English Poetry 1918–60
English Romantic Verse
English Verse
First World War Poetry
Georgian Poetry
Irish Verse
Light Verse
London in Verse
Love Poetry
The Metaphysical Poets
Modern African Poetry
Modern Arab Poetry
New Poetry
Poems of Science
Poetry of the Thirties
Post-War Russian Poetry
Spanish Civil War Verse
Unrespectable Verse
Urdu Poetry
Victorian Verse
Women Poets

Edward Albee   **Who's Afraid of Virginia Woolf?**

Alan Ayckbourn   **The Norman Conquests**

Bertolt Brecht   **Parables for the Theatre (The Good Woman of Setzuan/The Caucasian Chalk Circle)**

Anton Chekhov   **Plays (The Cherry Orchard/The Three Sisters/Ivanov/The Seagull/Uncle Vanya)**

Michael Hastings   **Tom and Viv**

Henrik Ibsen   **Hedda Gabler/Pillars of Society/The Wild Duck**

Eugène Ionesco   **Absurd Drama (Rhinoceros/The Chair/The Lesson)**

Ben Jonson   **Three Comedies (Volpone/The Alchemist/Bartholomew Fair)**

D. H. Lawrence   **Three Plays (The Collier's Friday Night/The Daughter-in-Law/The Widowing of Mrs Holroyd)**

Arthur Miller   **Death of a Salesman**

John Mortimer   **A Voyage Round My Father/What Shall We Tell Caroline?/The Dock Brief**

J. B. Priestley   **Time and the Conways/I Have Been Here Before/An Inspector Calls/The Linden Tree**

Peter Shaffer   **Amadeus**

Bernard Shaw   **Plays Pleasant (Arms and the Man/Candida/The Man of Destiny/You Never Can Tell)**

Sophocles   **Three Theban Plays (Oedipus the King/Antigone/Oedipus at Colonus)**

Arnold Wesker   **The Wesker Trilogy (Chicken Soup with Barley/Roots/I'm Talking about Jerusalem)**

Oscar Wilde   **Plays (Lady Windermere's Fan/A Woman of No Importance/An Ideal Husband/The Importance of Being Earnest/Salome)**

Thornton Wilder   **Our Town/The Skin of Our Teeth/The Matchmaker**

Tennessee Williams   **Sweet Bird of Youth/A Streetcar Named Desire/The Glass Menagerie**

The Collected Stories of Elizabeth Bowen

Seventy-nine stories – love stories, ghost stories, stories of childhood and of London during the Blitz – which all prove that 'the instinctive artist is there at the very heart of her work' – Angus Wilson

Tarr Wyndham Lewis

A strange picture of a grotesque world where human relationships are just fodder for a master race of artists, Lewis's extraordinary book remains 'a masterpiece of the period' – V. S. Pritchett

Chéri and The Last of Chéri Colette

Two novels that 'form the classic analysis of a love-affair between a very young man and a middle-aged woman' – Raymond Mortimer

Selected Poems 1923–1967 Jorge Luis Borges

A magnificent bilingual edition of the poetry of one of the greatest writers of today, conjuring up a unique world of invisible roses, uncaught tigers . . .

Beware of Pity Stefan Zweig

A cavalry officer becomes involved in the suffering of a young girl; when he attempts to avoid the consequences of his behaviour, the results prove fatal . . .

Valmouth and Other Novels Ronald Firbank

The world of Ronald Firbank – vibrant, colourful and fantastic – is to be found beneath soft deeps of velvet sky dotted with cognac clouds.

PENGUIN MODERN CLASSICS

Death of a Salesman Arthur Miller

One of the great American plays of the century, this classic study of failure brings to life an unforgettable character: Willy Loman, the shifting and inarticulate hero who is nonetheless a unique individual.

The Echoing Grove Rosamund Lehmann

'No English writer has told of the pains of women in love more truly or more movingly than Rosamund Lehmann' – Marghenita Laski. 'This novel is one of the most absorbing I have read for years' – Simon Raven, *Listener*

Pale Fire Vladimir Nabokov

This book contains the last poem by John Shade, together with a Preface, notes and Index by his posthumous editor. But is the eccentric editor more than just haughty and intolerant – mad, bad, perhaps even dangerous . . .?

The Man Who Was Thursday G. K. Chesterton

This hilarious extravaganza concerns a secret society of revolutionaries sworn to destroy the world. But when Thursday turns out to be not a poet but a Scotland Yard detective, one starts to wonder about the identity of the others . . .

The Rebel Albert Camus

Camus's attempt to understand 'the time I live in' tries to justify innocence in an age of atrocity. 'One of the vital works of our time, compassionate and disillusioned, intelligent but instructed by deeply felt experience' – *Observer*

Letters to Milena Franz Kafka

Perhaps the greatest collection of love letters written in the twentieth century, they are an orgy of bliss and despair, of ecstasy and desperation poured out by Kafka in his brief two-year relationship with Milena Jesenska.

FOR THE BEST IN PAPERBACKS, LOOK FOR THE 🐧

PENGUIN MODERN CLASSICS

The Age of Reason Jean-Paul Sartre

The first part of Sartre's classic trilogy, set in the volatile Paris summer of 1938, is itself 'a dynamic, deeply disturbing novel' (Elizabeth Bowen) which tackles some of the major issues of our time.

Three Lives Gertrude Stein

A turning point in American literature, these portraits of three women – thin, worn Anna, patient, gentle Lena and the complicated, intelligent Melanctha – represented in 1909 one of the pioneering examples of modernist writing.

Doctor Faustus Thomas Mann

Perhaps the most convincing description of an artistic genius ever written, this portrait of the composer Leverkuhn is a classic statement of one of Mann's obsessive themes: the discord between genius and sanity.

The New Machiavelli H. G. Wells

This autobiography of a man who has thrown up a glittering political career and marriage to go into exile with the woman he loves also contains an illuminating Introduction by Melvyn Bragg.

The Collected Poems of Stevie Smith

Amused, amusing and deliciously barbed, this volume includes many poems which dwell on death; as a whole, though, as this first complete edition in paperback makes clear, Smith's poetry affirms an irrepressible love of life.

Rhinoceros / The Chairs / The Lesson Eugène Ionesco

Three great plays by the man who was one of the founders of what has come to be known as the Theatre of the Absurd.

PENGUIN MODERN CLASSICS

The Second Sex   Simone de Beauvoir

This great study of Woman is a landmark in feminist history, drawing together insights from biology, history and sociology as well as literature, psychoanalysis and mythology to produce one of the supreme classics of the twentieth century.

The Bridge of San Luis Rey   Thornton Wilder

On 20 July 1714 the finest bridge in all Peru collapsed, killing 5 people. Why? Did it reveal a latent pattern in human life? In this beautiful, vivid and compassionate investigation, Wilder asks some searching questions in telling the story of the survivors.

Parents and Children   Ivy Compton-Burnett

This richly entertaining introduction to the world of a unique novelist brings to light the deadly claustrophobia within a late-Victorian upper-middle-class family . . .

Vienna 1900   Arthur Schnitzler

These deceptively languid sketches, four 'games with love and death', lay bare an astonishing and disturbing world of sexual turmoil (which anticipates Freud's discoveries) beneath the smooth surface of manners and convention.

Confessions of Zeno   Italo Svevo

Zeno, an innocent in a corrupt world, triumphs in the end through his stoic acceptance of his own failings in this extraordinary, experimental novel which fuses memory, obsession and desire.

The House of Mirth   Edith Wharton

Lily Bart – beautiful, intelligent and charming – is trapped like a butterfly in the inverted jam jar of wealthy New York society . . . This tragic comedy of manners was one of Wharton's most shocking and innovative books.